Chasing
the
Dream:
A Player's Guide

by

TRACY McPHEE

Published by

 GENERAL STORE
PUBLISHING HOUSE

Box 28, 1694 Burnstown Road,
Burnstown, Ontario, Canada K0J 1G0
Telephone (613) 432-7697 or 1-800-465-6072

ISBN 1-894263-01-4
Printed and bound in Canada
Copyright 1999

Layout and Design by Derek McEwen
Printing by Custom Printers of Renfrew Ltd.

General Store Publishing House
Burnstown, Ontario, Canada

Canadian Cataloguing in Publication Data

McPhee, Tracy, 1971-
  Chasing the dream : a player's guide

ISBN 1-894263-01-4

  I. Hockey. I. Title.

GV847.M34 1999   796.962   C99-901432-3

Dedication

This book is dedicated to an important person, my father, Norman McPhee. He was a skilled player when he was younger, a patient and enthusiastic volunteer coach for minor hockey and a loyal Montreal Canadiens fan. Everything I know about appreciating what hockey is to Canadians I learned from him.

Acknowledgements

I want to thank all the people—players, coaches, scouts, doctors, agents, trainers, and instructors—who shared their experiences for the book. Everyone had hectic schedules and made the extra effort to be available. Since most of these people are listed in the book I won't repeat their names but I do want them to know I really appreciate their contribution.

I would also like to add a thank you to some people who aren't in the book. I appreciate the information and pictures provided by the CHL teams. I would especially like to thank Dave Lord (CHL), Karen Ruttan (CHL—St. Clair group), Ted Baker (OHL), Lloyd Hamshaw (WHL) and Gilles Courteau (QMJHL) for providing the information about the leagues. A special thanks to Dan Hamilton who made the extra effort to go out and get some additional pictures so I could have the cover I wanted.

I want to thank Roy McGregor for helping me pull the pieces together and my editors, John Stevens and Vicki Cameron, for their work on the manuscript.

Mike Schaab, Caroline Hassard, and RJ Moorehouse, thank you for recommending some of the people I spoke to for the book. Thanks as well to Sandy Sutton and Meredith Gill for their assistance in proof-reading the manuscript. Thanks to Lorraine McPhee, Nolan McPhee, Lori King, and Renée Touesnard for trying to get exposure for the book before it was even published.

A very special thank you to Cathy Markson and Christa Hellstrom for keeping me motivated. Thank you for believing in me and keeping me going when I got frustrated.

Table of Contents

Chapter 1
HOCKEY DREAMS

YOUNG HOCKEY PLAYERS grow up playing on ponds and backyard rinks. Alone on the ice with a stick and the sound of their blades cutting the ice they hear the roar of a phantom crowd. It's a breakaway, the shot, the goal. In the imaginary roar of the crowd they hoist their sticks in triumph or maybe fire off a sharp Jagr-like salute.

For the fortunate few the dream of playing in the NHL will become a reality. It will not come easily. Even the most talented players will feel the frustration of a bad season or buckle under the intense media scrutiny that accompanies such talent. The reality of being a professional hockey player must be pursued with a diligence and discipline that can only be achieved out of a true and lasting love of Canada's national obsession.

The realization of the dream requires the player to move from the local arena to a venue where scouts will come, see and draft. There are only a few routes into the NHL and the fastest route is the Canadian Hockey League (CHL).

In fifty-four cities across Canada and the United States young hockey hopefuls play game after game in a demanding, high profile, high pressure league. This book gives young players a glimpse at life in Canada's elite Major Junior hockey league and some guidance on getting there and staying there.

TAKING IT TO THE NEXT LEVEL: PLAYING IN THE CHL

So What Is This League?

The Canadian Hockey League (CHL) is the governing body for Major Junior "A" hockey. The CHL encompasses the three leagues that make up this elite system, the Western Hockey League (WHL),

Ontario Hockey League (OHL) and Quebec Major Junior Hockey League (QMJHL). Although there are similarities among the leagues, they are distinct. Teams from the three leagues meet at the end of the season to battle for the coveted Memorial Cup.

In 1997-98 there were fifty-one teams in the league. The number expanded in the 1998-99 season when two new OHL teams hit the ice. Expansion is a common occurrence in the leagues. Since the 1990-91 season the CHL has expanded by thirteen teams. In addition to newly created teams, some teams have packed up and moved to new locations. The new Cape Breton Screaming Eagles are actually the renamed and relocated Granby Predateurs.

The league is spread throughout eight provinces and four states. This can make for some pretty big moves and pretty long road trips for the players, who are typically between the ages of seventeen and nineteen during their stints in Major Junior. Teams are allowed to carry some sixteen-year-olds and a limited number of "overage" twenty-year-olds.

The CHL is the largest hockey league in the world and it is a proving ground for young hockey prospects, players with the potential to continue on into the NHL. It is not an easy road for young players. It can be tough to make a CHL team and even tougher to develop into an NHL prospect.

Many players look to the CHL as a big step in pursuit of their hockey dreams. It is a big step and one that few players make. The CHL, like the NHL, is a league where players are invited to attend. This is a coveted and hard-to-come-by invitation. Players are either drafted by a team or invited to attend training camp. The process is driven by the team's needs.

Later chapters will examine some of the qualities that teams and scouts look for in a prospect but there is no formula that equals a CHL-calibre player. Players and sometimes parents obsess about exposure, being scouted and getting that opportunity. The scouts are out there and they are looking for the talented few who have the qualities and drive to play in the NHL.

Some players are late bloomers; some players are too small; some players have potential that never pans out. Even players who appear great in a small community must be aware that they are competing against players from all over Canada, the United States and a small pool of Europeans. Players should focus on enjoying the game and playing to the best of their ability. This book looks at the realities of the league for those players talented and fortunate enough to get the invitations.

2

Chasing the Dream All Over Western Canada: Donovan Nunweiller

Donovan Nunweiller is a young player who grew up knowing he wanted to play in the CHL. He discovered that getting there would be a long and occasionally heartbreaking journey.

Donovan grew up playing hockey in Redcliff, Alberta. He was an avid fan of the local CHL team, the Medicine Hat Tigers, and dreamed of one day donning that jersey. He knew it would be an important step towards his dream of a future in the NHL.

Despite being overlooked in the Bantam Draft the young goalie got an invitation to the Tigers' training camp. A solid performance earned him a spot on the team's fifty-player protected list when he was fifteen. Unfortunately, the team had strong goaltending and Donovan could not crack the lineup that year. He went down to his Bantam AAA Team but he had every intention of coming back up.

Up . . . and Back . . . and Up . . . and Back . . .

He did come back to camp. When he was sixteen, when he was seventeen and again when he was eighteen. Each time at the end of camp, he was sent back down. It was a frustrating and disappointing time. He was on the Tigers' protected list but he could not get the team to play him or trade him.

The toughest year for Donovan was when he was seventeen. He trained really hard. He exercised, he practiced, he ate right. He had never wanted to make the team more and he was cut. It was one of the most discouraging moments of his fledgling hockey career. He put everything he had into preparing for that year and it was not enough. Discouraged and depressed he went home. What did he need to do to get a shot in nets in this league . . . eat the pucks?

Donovan admits it is very difficult not being in control of your future. You only get to play if someone else decides to let you. You do get desperate when you turn nineteen or twenty and think you are never going to get an opportunity. Hockey is a time-driven profession and you need to get the window of opportunity early.

Have Pads, Will Travel

Despite being cut the previous season, Donovan returned at eighteen, ready to play and a little scared that he was never going to get his chance. He was doing well but the team did not need another goalie. Other teams expressed an interest and the Tigers sent Donovan to the Swift Current Broncos for the exhibition season. If the Broncos liked him, the team would arrange a trade. Donovan was with the team for about three weeks. The team decided to pass so the Tigers, who were still trying to find a trade for Donovan, sent him to Kamloops.

Donovan packed up his car and headed west. He did one practice with the Blazers before being told they would also pass. Feeling slightly rejected but still determined, Donovan packed up and headed for his next audition. This time he headed east to Lethbridge. He managed three weeks there before the team decided to pass.

The dejected young netminder finally packed up his pads and headed home. This was a dark time for him. It looked like his dream of playing in the NHL was getting further away. He credits his family with giving him the support he needed to get through it. When he returned home, he called Humboldt, the team that held his minor league hockey rights, to see if he could get back in the game. The team told him they wanted him to come back but they wanted him to call again before he came. After two months of driving around western Canada, Donovan knew a trade when he smelled it.

This time his rights were traded to Melville, Saskatchewan. Donovan packed up his little red Nissan and headed for his new team. He was trade-shy by this time. Like many players he is also a bit superstitious. Unpacking might jinx him, so he didn't. Donovan only unpacked his car after the trade deadline passed.

Donovan's job search was a discouraging experience. His confidence was low but he stuck it out. The teams were nice to him, they each took care of him during his time with them and made sure he had a stipend and gas money. There were just no takers. Donovan admits being a goaltender is a tough position. Each team has only two and if you happen to hit a year with some strong starters it is hard to crack the lineup.

Getting By With a Little Help From Your Friends

Donovan credits the support from his family and friends as a critical factor in toughing out the setbacks and rejections. Since he was nineteen when he finally cracked the league he did not leave his friends behind. They were already in university and he was home alone. Donovan's friends were encouraging. They readily admitted that if they had had the opportunity they would have kept trying.

Watching a son deal with rejection and frustration is not easy for parents. Donovan's parents did not push him to keep playing and they did not try to persuade him to give up and go to university. Hockey was Donovan's dream for as long as he wanted to pursue it and his parents respected that.

Once he made the decision to play, his parents did everything they could to support him. This support translated to lots of phone calls to Melville, Saskatchewan. It also meant some long nights for Donovan's dad. Donovan's confidence was so low by the time he joined Melville that he was letting in some pretty weak shots. Donovan's father, Donald, would drive six and a half hours to watch Donovan play and then make the return drive through the night to be at work the next morning. This support got Donovan through a tough season.

Getting the Job

Donovan got an invitation to attend the Moose Jaw Warriors' training camp. Still determined to make it into the CHL the 19-year-old netminder headed to Moose Jaw. This time it clicked for the player and he managed to earn a spot on the roster, earn it and keep it by an outstanding performance. He recorded six shut-outs during his first season, tying Felix Potvin's CHL record. Donovan proved he had what it takes when in his rookie year he was named to the Western Hockey League's first all star team and earned Rookie of the Year honours.

On Playing In the League

Donovan is not embittered by his difficulties in getting a spot on a CHL roster. The quality of the players trying out for the league means that it is tough to earn a spot. His rocky start has made him realize the importance of mental toughness.

Donovan tries to encourage younger players when they get sent down or do not make the cut at camp. He knows first hand the frustration and disappointment a young player can face. To make it you have to believe in yourself, dig in and keep working.

Donovan Nunweiller, No. 35
Moose Jaw Warriors
*Photograph courtesy of the Moose Jaw
Warriors Hockey Club*

Where the Players Are

Was Donovan's dogged pursuit of a spot on a CHL roster worth it? His friends assured him it was. A tenacity that would have impressed a pit bull kept him coming back, but the question is why? What does this league offer that draws thousands of hockey hopefuls to its training camps every year?

Top NHL stars cut their hockey teeth (or what is left of them) in this league and every year young players vie for spots on CHL teams' rosters. The league can be a tough transition for a young athlete. The player usually has to move to a new city and a new home. There is a rigorous game schedule, regular practices and lots of time on the bus. So why do players do it?

Donovan believes the CHL is a great developmental league for players. This is a belief he shares with scouts and coaches. Former Canucks Coach Tom Renney likens the CHL to an infant NHL and former Leafs scout Dan Marr called it a hockey prep school. The hectic game and travel schedule is as much preparation for an NHL future as the hockey itself. The quality of the players in the league creates a high level of competition and players are challenged to improve their game to meet the demands of the league.

CHOOSING THE CHL: PLAYERS' PERSPECTIVES

Jay Henderson, Edmonton Ice

The players come for more than the ice time and tough play. Edmonton Ice's Jay Henderson knew that the WHL gave young players a chance to be in the spotlight and that was the place to be if you had hopes of being drafted by an NHL team. Jay did some research on the league before he made his decision.

The WHL had a good scholarship package and the team stressed education so he knew he would come out academically sound if hockey did not pan out. He did get some offers to play college hockey in the United States but decided that Major Junior was the league for him.

The intensity and focus on hockey that the WHL offered appealed to Jay and influenced his decision to go this route, a route he figured would be the fastest to the NHL. Jay made the decision to play Major Junior on his own but his family supported his decision to play for the Red Deer Rebels.

Jay was motivated to excel by a teacher. The teacher laughed at his dream of playing professional hockey. It looks like this WHL All-Star prospect had the last laugh. Despite being a low round pick in the NHL draft (OK dead last), Jay Henderson has signed an NHL contract. In the 1998-99 season that teacher could catch Jay on Hockey Night in

6

Canada as he learned to go from prospect to player with the Boston Bruins.

Colin White, Hull Olympiques

Not all players grow up hoping to play in the CHL. Colin White grew up not knowing about the league. The Major Junior league had not spread to Nova Scotia yet and the New Glasgow native finally heard about the league in his draft year. During that year Colin began to receive phone calls and spoke to scouts from CHL teams. There was considerable interest in the promising young defenceman.

When he learned about the league Colin liked what he heard. The quality of former players and the number of current players being drafted out of the league made it the place to be for a prospect. Colin was excited to be drafted into the QMJHL and made the trip to Laval to play. With the Moose loose on the mainland and the Eagles Screaming in Cape Breton young Nova Scotians are now growing up with plenty of exposure to the CHL.

New Jersey's second round pick in the 1996 Entry Draft, Colin now plays with the Albany River Rats, the New Jersey Devil's farm team. Major Junior developed Colin as a player and he also credits the league with preparing him for the lifestyle. The frequent travel and discipline were excellent training for a future in hockey. Colin's new team does not impose curfews and Colin no longer billets but he developed habits in junior that keep him focused in a demanding profession.

Craig Hillier, Ottawa 67's

From the time he knew what it was, Ottawa 67's netminder Craig Hillier wanted to play in the NHL. In his fourth and final year with the 67's Craig credits the league with bringing him closer to his dream.

Craig did not know much about the league when he was a young player. He did know that it was the fastest way to the NHL. He knew the odds were against him and that only a small percentage of players actually make it. He did not care, since his focus was always on looking straight forward to the NHL.

Craig had already received information packages from National Collegiate Athletic Association (NCAA) teams but he wanted to play Major Junior. The NCAA was a last resort. If Craig was overlooked by the CHL teams in their entrance drafts, he had decided to find a Tier II team in Ontario to wait for next year. As a seventeen-year-old he would have had a better chance of being drafted into the CHL.

Craig Hillier, No. 30 – Ottawa 67's
Photograph courtesy of Gaëton Bourbonnais

When Craig was sixteen, Nova Scotian players could go in either the OHL or QMJHL Drafts. The OHL drafts older players and to make it that year Craig would have had to be drafted as an under-age player. This meant he would have had to be selected in the first three rounds. An oversight left Craig off the QMJHL list, an oversight that would have Quebec teams kicking themselves when Craig developed into a top CHL goaltender. Craig had no choice but to look to the OHL.

Fortunately, he was drawing some interest from OHL teams. Ottawa, Oshawa and London were all taking a careful look at the sixteen-year-old goaltender. Craig was also doing some research on the league. He and his parents sat down with Halifax native Mike Johnson and his family to discuss his stint in the OHL. Craig liked what he heard.

The league offered an intense focus on hockey and lots of exposure for a young prospect hoping to be drafted to the NHL. By the time he was drafted by the 67's, Craig had a better idea of what to expect in terms of game schedules and billeting.

The actual play was still a big surprise; the quality of the players was a clear indication of the rapid development in the league and it was a big step even for a talented rookie. However, players do adjust to the

8

lifestyle and pick up their game. Craig thrived in the league, becoming a top rated goalie and Pittsburgh's first round pick in 1996.

A LOOK AT THE STATS

Does the CHL deliver on the promise of hockey stardom? A look at the NHL reveals that former CHL players dominate NHL rosters. In the 1997-98 season approximately sixty-five percent of the players on NHL teams were former CHL players. Superstars like Wayne Gretzky, Mark Messier, Mario Lemieux, Joe Sakic, Patrick Roy, Steve Yzerman, Felix Potvin, Pat Lafontaine, and Eric Lindros got their starts in this elite league.

That was then, but what about today? Is the CHL still the fast track to a professional career? The dynamics of hockey is changing as more Americans and Europeans enter the sport. Statistically the percentage of CHL players being drafted has decreased in recent years. The biggest increase in players is young Europeans who are following in the footsteps of players like Hasek, Sundin, Federov, and Selanne.

Despite these changes, the CHL still provided more than half the players in the 1997 Entry Draft (fifty-four percent, to be exact). First round selections heavily favoured the CHL with nineteen of the twenty-six prospects coming from this league. The high quality of the players is reflected by the fact that seventy-one percent of all the players drafted in the first two rounds came from the CHL.

LOOKING AHEAD

Despite the impressive number of former players in the NHL, this still represents only a small portion of all the players who have donned CHL jerseys. An NHL dream is a hard-won reality. Many talented young players end their hockey careers in this league without ever getting a crack at NHL ice.

For some of these players, opportunities in countries like Germany and Japan, or in America's new minor pro leagues, can extend their careers but it is not THE DREAM. Other players take their CHL scholarship packages and head to university.

Even after a stellar season Donovan cannot relax and coast into an NHL future. Despite his outstanding performance Donovan was overlooked in the NHL Entry Draft. He still looks to the NHL as a free agent but not being drafted was heartbreaking.

At 5'10" Donovan will have to deal with the "Size is Everything" mentality that pervades the NHL. He admits to being disappointed that he failed to get an invitation to an NHL camp after what was probably the best season of his career. He feels he can take his game to the next level but he needs the opportunity to do that. After two years of chasing a spot on a CHL roster Donovan is not about to give up his dream of a spot on an NHL roster.

The following three chapters provide players with a brief introduction to the three leagues that make up the CHL; and profile some young prospects who are starting their professional careers.

Chapter 2
THE QUEBEC MAJOR JUNIOR HOCKEY LEAGUE (QMJHL)

THE QUEBEC MAJOR JUNIOR HOCKEY LEAGUE is in its twenty-ninth year as an elite hockey league. Founded in 1969, the league resulted from a merger between the provincial Junior "A" league and the metropolitan league. There are currently sixteen teams in the "Q". A new team in Montreal joined the league in 1999-2000 and brought the CHL back to this city. The Montreal Rockets will play out of the Maurice Richard Arena.

The league expanded into the Maritimes in 1994 and boasts teams in New Brunswick and Nova Scotia. The league is divided into two divisions; most of the regular season games are played within the division.

The Robert LeBel Division	The Frank-Dilio Division
Drummondville Voltigeurs	Baie-Comeau Drakkar
Hull Olympiques	Cape Breton Screaming Eagles
Acadie-Bathurst Titans	Chicoutimi Sagueneens
Rouyn-Noranda Huskies	Halifax Mooseheads
Shawinigan Cataractes	Moncton Wildcats
Sherbrooke Castors	Quebec Remparts
Val d'Or Foreurs	Rimouski Oceanics
Victoriaville Tigers	

• For an introduction to these cities and their teams see the Reference Section at the end of the book.

11

PLAYER IN PROFILE: JEAN-SEBASTIEN "GIGER" GIGUERE

A look at the leagues means more than just learning about the teams. The players are the most important part of the league. Jean-Sebastien Giguere is a CHL player who has graduated and moved on to a professional career but he shares his memories of his time in the league.

Like many young Canadians, Jean-Sebastien was on the ice before he could lace his own skates. Figure skating at three, hockey at four and between the pipes at five, this young goalie found his calling early. And yes, the initial attraction was the cool equipment.

Jean-Sebastien is one of five hockey-playing siblings. Older brother Stephan did a stint in the QMJHL and in the IHL. Alain Giguere was also a talented young player. One of the Giguere siblings went to the 1998 Olympics in Nagano, Japan, but not as a competitor. Sister Isabelle is a referee and has even made the calls when little brother was on the ice. During the 1995-96 World Junior training camp, Isabelle was a referee. Jean-Sebastien's other sister Caroline logged some ice time with NHL netminder Jocelyn Thibault as a minor league player.

Claude and Giselle Giguere were definitely bringing up a hockey family in their home in Blainville, Quebec. This Montreal suburb is only fifteen minutes from downtown. Despite the proximity to Montreal, young Jean-Sebastien grew up a Nordiques fan.

Jean-Sebastien's love of hockey may be a family tradition but his talent and commitment have made it a calling. Except for the occasional game of street hockey the young goaltender has always found a home between the pipes.

On the Game

"I guess every year it is a new challenge. You have a goal; I wanted to make the big team. The feeling you have when you win a big game, it's unbelievable. There is no better feeling than that."

On the Position

Giguere has logged a lot of years in the net. He was a starting goaltender for three years with the Halifax Mooseheads. He shared net duties while he was with the Calgary Flames farm team in Saint John, NB. Despite his front and centre role, he does remember what it is like to be a back-up goaltender.

"When you are a back-up goalie you always have to be ready, mentally and physically." Giguere concedes that you do lose a bit of motivation when you are a back-up goalie. When you are a player you love to play but being a back-up is part of being a goaltender.

What about when you are the starting goaltender? According to Giguere the hardest part is keeping that mental edge, period after period, game after game. Goaltending is an exercise in endurance and concentration. The other players are on and off the ice but as a goaltender you are in for the long haul. You have to be in good shape to do this. Giguere stays in shape by biking during the summer. He also does exercises to develop his leg strength.

On Keeping the Puck Out Of the Net

Giguere likes to keep the options narrow for players. He puts himself directly between the puck and the net. With 6'2" and 170 pounds of goalie in the way, a player coming in is going to have a tough time finding an opening. Though not as flashy as some of the more spectacular saves, this method has been effective for the young goalie.

On the League

When the time came, Giguere was definitely going to the QMJHL. His brother's stint in the league let Giguere know what to expect and he thought it was the best option. It was a developmental league and he wanted to develop. Drafted at fifteen, his first year in the league saw Giguere play in Verdun, Quebec. The team was part of a school and the players lived in a dormitory while they played for the team. The team was shaky when Giguere joined. There were rumours it would fold. Early in the year the team learned this year would be the last.

Did the rookie goaltender know where he would be heading at the end of the year? He had a hunch that the new Halifax Mooseheads might pick him up from the league. He was right. How could an expansion team pass on Verdun's rookie of the year?

Halifax came to see Giguere and get a feel for whether the French player could make a home in an English-speaking city. Despite a low mark in his English class Giguere was anxious to join the team. This rookie's sights were already set on a predominately English-speaking NHL. He wanted to improve his English.

Coach Jodoin was bilingual but the team operated in English. Giguere could have requested a bilingual billet but he knew that would only slow down his learning process. He admits adjusting to living in an English-speaking city was tough at first. At training camp the team was pretty much divided along language lines. This changed quickly as the team started to play and the players adjusted to their home in Halifax. The French players picked up English quickly.

Billeting was no problem for Giguere. It was a bit strange at first but the people were friendly. He notes that the Maritime reputation for friendliness is well-deserved. The food was a definite improvement over the food at the school's residence. Like most players he found he had fewer responsibilities when he was billeting. Being accustomed to doing his own cooking and cleaning, he found it an adjustment.

Even road trips, usually a source of complaint for young players, were OK by Giguere. The long trips give players a chance to get to know one another off the ice. Giguere looks back fondly on the mileage he logged with his junior team.

The Fledgling Team

Giguere was busy during his years with Halifax. The young team was finding its feet and that meant a lot of shots on goal. Giguere faced an average of thirty-seven shots per game. Did the pressure bother the young netminder? Giguere found that getting so many shots meant he was challenged to improve his game. "I like being the last line of defense. I like it when the team relies on me."

Jean-Sebastien Giguere, No. 47 – Halifax Mooseheads
Photographs courtesy of Terry Waterfield

The Playoff Challenge

The 1996-97 season was a big one for the fledgling Mooseheads. After a slow start the 1994 expansion team was geared up for a playoff run. Jean-Sebastien has great memories of that season. The team was playing well and winning and it was a great feeling even though they suffered a heartbreaking seventh-game loss to Chicoutimi in the divisional finals.

On Getting Drafted

Did the first goalie to go in the 1995 NHL draft know it was going to happen? No. When he started his draft-eligible season Giguere was motivated. He wanted to be drafted. He didn't care where, when or by whom. Heading into draft day Giguere had a hunch he was going to go. Maybe second round or even late first round. Fellow netminder Martin Biron was also on the block for this draft.

Giguere met with about ten teams during the season, some early in the year and three or four the night before the draft. Giguere admits it was quite a process. You had to mingle and it was anything but casual for the young prospects. Every player wore his best suit and his best manners. There were lots of big league guys there and you didn't want to look or sound stupid.

Giguere was very thankful his English had improved so dramatically; it made the process easier. He met with the Whalers the night before the July 6th, 1995 draft. His advice on the interview: it is no place for false modesty. You have to be confident and you have to show it.

The rumour mill was high on Biron but Giguere trusted his abilities and when the Whalers asked him who was better he swallowed any doubts and said he was. They must have believed him because the next day they made Jean-Sebastien the first goalie to go, thirteenth overall in the 1995 draft.

Sitting with his parents and girlfriend in the Edmonton Coliseum, Giguere didn't even hear his own name. He was still waiting to see when Biron would draft. Fortunately Dad was paying more attention. The thrilled parents sent their youngest son down to the podium to collect his jersey. Traditionally thirteen is not a lucky number but it will always be a memorable one for this young goaltender.

On Camps

Giguere attended two camps with Hartford. His first camp was nothing spectacular. He admits he felt a certain amount of intimidation about going to camp. That is natural when you hit the ice with seasoned

NHL players. Jean-Sebastien is a quiet guy and it took him a while to loosen up. He gave a better performance the second year, certainly a more impressive performance than his first year.

On the Call

After being drafted Giguere signed a contract and went back to work with his major junior team. That is a pretty typical scenario for young players. What is not so typical is getting called up. Giguere got called into the office one day by his coach. A dislocated thumb had left the Whalers in the lurch and they needed Giguere. He had got the call . . . he was going up. Way up.

He barely had time to pack before he caught a plane to catch up with his team. Thinking he would be there for maybe a week Giguere packed light. The week turned into a month and a half. Luckily, he got his first paycheck, and shopping for a few things was not a problem.

The first two weeks on the job Giguere was a back-up. He was not a reserve. During his sixteen games with the team he played in eight. He logged one win and four losses during his stint. Giguere admits it was a big step up for him but the experience was amazing.

The First Game

Giguere was a back-up goalie in his first game. Unfortunately, there was no room on the bench and he spent his first game in the stands. You would think that a back-up goalie would at least get a good view of the game even if he didn't get to play. Unfortunately many benches don't accommodate the bulk of a suited-up goalie very well and the back-ups are often forced into makeshift seating arrangements. It was an away game and Giguere took some ribbing from the fans. Maybe you can at least get some snacks if you are stuck in the stands.

Biggest Moment

Giguere did not spend all his time on the bench. He did see action as Hartford's netminder. In Giguere's case his most vivid memory wasn't the shot he blocked or the game he won. Ten minutes into a game against the New York Rangers Giguere joined an illustrious alumni of netminders. He was beaten by the Great One. Giguere doesn't like being scored on but he admits that giving up a goal to Gretzky was "unbelievable." It was a scrapbook memory for a Canadian kid.

The Trade

Giguere's stint with the Hartford Whalers, now the Carolina Hurricanes, came to an end with a pre-season trade to the Calgary

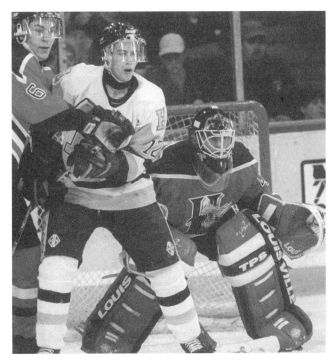

Jean-Sebastien Giguere, No. 47
Halifax Mooseheads
Photographs courtesy of Terry Waterfield

Flames. The biggest disappointment for the young netminder was that the trade came before an exhibition game scheduled to take place in Halifax, NS. With former teammates and friends in the city the game would have been an emotional one. His impression of Calgary: a great hockey city with amazing fans, although he jokingly acknowledges that Carolina would be warmer.

Giguere had got to know the Hartford/Carolina players after his five-week stint with the team. He knew he would have to work at building a reputation with his new team. A quiet guy, Giguere lets his work ethic and talent speak for him.

The Saint John Flames

Sent to the Flames farm team in Saint John, NB, the young netminder found himself back in the Maritimes. Jean-Sebastien likes the city, it reminds him of Halifax. No more billeting for this young player; he and a teammate have their own place. Jean-Sebastien is looking forward to getting as much playing time as possible during his stint in the American Hockey League (AHL).

Playing In the NHL

The Saint John Flames had to do without Giguere and fellow AHL netminder Tyler Moss when injuries left both of the Calgary Flames goaltenders sidelined. At the start of the 1998-99 season Giguere and Moss shared duties as Calgary's backstop. Giguere likes to play the tough games and this stint will certainly give him that opportunity.

On a Personal Note

Yes, there is life off the ice. When Giguere isn't on the road, on the ice or at the gym he likes to relax by watching movies. His favourite is *Shawshank Redemption*. He is also an enthusiastic racquet ball player and with his hand-eye coordination is a tough player to get the ball past.

The netminder's favourite hockey player is recent Hall of Fame inductee Mario Lemieux. His music of choice is Our Lady Peace, a band he bought tickets to see when he had a rare break in his hectic schedule. When it comes time to chow down he shares the tastes of Garfield the cat. He is always willing to scarf down the nearest available lasagna.

Jean-Sebastien Giguere,
No. 47
Calgary Flames
*Photograph courtesy of Dan
Hamilton, Vantage Point Studios*

Chapter 3
THE ONTARIO HOCKEY LEAGUE (OHL)

HOCKEY IN ONTARIO has a long history. The first association, the Ontario Hockey Association, was formed on November 27th, 1890. It was not until the 1970s that major junior hockey was recognized. The league was operating out of the Ontario Hockey Association Office (OHA). In 1974 the teams' owners established the office of the Commissioner and changed the name to the Ontario Major Junior Hockey League. The name was changed to its current variation in 1981 when it became the Ontario Hockey League.

The league, despite its name, has spread beyond the boundaries of the province. The league boasts two American franchises, the Erie Otters of Erie, Pennsylvania and the Plymouth Whalers of Plymouth, Michigan. There are currently twenty teams in the OHL. The league restructured from two divisions to four to accommodate its growth in the 1998-99 season.

EASTERN CONFERENCE		WESTERN CONFERENCE	
East	*Central*	*Midwest*	*West*
Belleville Bulls	Barrie Colts	Erie Otters	London Knights
Kingston Frontenacs	Mississauga Ice Dogs	Brampton Battalion	Plymouth Whalers
Oshawa Generals	North Bay Centennials	Guelph Storm	Sarnia Sting
Ottawa 67's	Sudbury	Kitchener Rangers	Sault St. Marie Greyhounds
Peterborough Petes	St. Mike's Majors	Owen Sound Platers	Windsor Spitfires

• **For an introduction to the cities and teams see the reference section at the end of the book.**

PLAYER IN PROFILE: ALYN "MAC" McCAULEY

Alyn McCauley hit the ice at a young age. He was only two when he learned to skate and he was playing organized hockey by four. In Alyn's home town of Gananoque, a small community on the St. Lawrence River, hockey is a popular pastime. The only boy in the family, Alyn has one sister, Amber. His parents are enthusiastic supporters of Alyn's game.

On the Game

Always a competitive guy, Alyn found hockey gave him a battleground and an opponent to conquer. He has always loved the game and like any elite player he plays to win, every game. He is quick to note that "nothing compares to the intensity and focus you get when you hit the ice."

Being a Centre

Like many young players, Alyn experimented with positions during his minor hockey days. He even logged some time in the net. Unfortunately, he could not get the hang of it and after giving up thirteen goals in a game, the team found a new spot for him. Once he got the pads off he managed a ten-point game. That was the end of any goaltending ambitions and the beginning of a career as a points producer.

So what does this guy do to record 112 points in a single regular season? Well, Alyn characterizes himself as a smart player. He tries to be aware of the players on the ice and his position. Alyn's advice is to "study your own end, your defensive play, and just let the offence take care of itself."

Deciding On the OHL

As an exceptional young player, Alyn advanced quickly and was already playing Tier II when he became eligible to play in the OHL. He did consider NCAA teams but felt that if he waited for NCAA he would not be developing.

Alyn's agent and parents were very supportive and helpful but the ultimate decision was Alyn's. The OHL would offer Alyn a chance to showcase his talents, an opportunity that might help him realize his dream of one day playing in the NHL. If you are wondering if it worked, you can catch Alyn on Hockey Night in Canada whenever the Leafs are playing.

When it came to the game, Alyn expected the OHL to be a good blend between toughness and skill. After four years in the league Alyn confirms that is exactly what he got.

Making the Move

Decision made, there was no lack of interest in this young prospect. The Ottawa 67's snapped up the young forward first overall in the 1993 OHL Priority Draft. The hardest adjustment Alyn made as a young player was getting comfortable in his new environment. Moving away from home is tough, adjusting to living with a new family and playing with a new team make it tougher. Alyn's a quiet guy. He took his time getting to know his billet family and his new teammates.

After he made the initial adjustment Alyn became close to his billet

Alyn McCauley, No. 18
Ottawa 67's
Photograph courtesy of Gaetan Bourbonnais

family. He spent all four years with the Mathieu family and credits them with making his adjustment an easier one. Although he has moved on he still keeps in touch with the family. Alyn likes school as much as the next guy, but he definitely recognizes the importance of education. He finished high school while he was in Ottawa and is planning to take some university courses. Math is his best subject and he intends to take some accounting courses.

Playing In the League

The seventy-plus game season was a long haul for a rookie. As Alyn became more comfortable in the league he adjusted to the hectic schedule. At first he struggled to keep up but he got into a routine and the season passed more quickly.

As a top-rated prospect Alyn saw lots of ice even during his rookie season. He admits he thought it would be easier. He was used to being a high scorer. In junior, he had to work harder to put the puck into the net.

Like all CHL teams the Ottawa 67's logged time on the road. You have to find ways to pass the time. In his second year, Alyn took up a new hobby, chess. A player with a strong sense of strategy, Alyn got hooked on the game. The players brought along tiny travel boards with magnetic pieces. He also likes to do crossword puzzles to pass the long hours on the bus and, more recently, on the plane.

A Tough Year

Alyn's list of accomplishments is impressive. He was a two-time member of gold-winning National junior teams. He won the prestigious CHL's 1996-97 Player of the Year award in his last season in the league. With 112 regular season points and thirty-six playoff points it was a noteworthy season for the 67's captain.

These accomplishments came after a very tough season. The 1994-95 season was supposed to be a big year for Alyn. He was draft-eligible and that is a high pressure time for any player with NHL dreams. The season got off to a bad start. Eight of his goals were disallowed, leaving Alyn frustrated and pointless. Eventually, he scored allowed goals but the eight lost goals left his numbers looking a little low.

Even with the slow start, Alyn recorded fifty-four points that season. Unfortunately, as a first pick in the OHL draft, more was expected. The press was tough on Alyn during that season and that is hard on a young player. Alyn questioned his dream that season but instead of giving in to the frustration, he dug in and decided to prove the doubters wrong.

On the Draft

The 1995 NHL Entry Draft saw Alyn go in the fourth round when New Jersey picked him up seventy-ninth overall. The team got a bargain. Alyn admits that the fourth round selection was a huge blow. In retrospect it may have helped him. It gave him the motivation to excel.

Players react differently to the draft. Some high round selections relax and act as if they are going to have an easy ride, others are pumped and work even harder. Alyn knew that he was a better player, and he set out to prove it. He did it with style as he rebounded from that season to walk away from the CHL as the Player of the Year.

After the draft Alyn spent the summer working for his dad in his painting business during the day and working out in the evening. The seventeen-hour days were part of his commitment to proving himself. The summer also helped him refocus on hockey as a career. He knew

Alyn McCauley, No.18
World Junior Tournament
Photograph Courtesy of the Canadian Hockey Association

that being selected into the draft was no guarantee of an NHL future. Alyn was ready to re-join the 67's and have a stellar season.

When You Are Winning

Alyn's final season with the Ottawa 67's was an amazing experience. The team just clicked. Everything seemed to be working for them. Under the leadership of Coach Brian "Killer" Kilrea, the team was first in the league for all but a couple of weeks during the regular season.

World Junior Tournament

Another career highlight for Alyn was back-to-back gold medals at the World Junior Tournament. Alyn first earned a spot on the National Junior team for the 1996 Tournament in Boston. He was thrilled to make the roster and represent Canada. The fact that the tournament was being held in Boston allowed family and friends to make the trip. Sharing the gold-winning experience with his family was very special.

The win did not make Alyn less hungry for a repeat in the 1997 Tournament in Geneva, Switzerland. If anything he was more focused. As the Assistant Captain he also tried to step up and provide leadership to the team, a task that was made more difficult by a bout of bronchitis. For the first few days after arriving in Europe, Alyn was flat on his back trying to recover. He rallied quickly and won a pivotal faceoff for the team in the gold medal game against the United States.

Life After Junior

Alyn left junior with a bang and he started his NHL career the same way. He was part of the trade that saw former Leafs' Captain Doug Gilmour go to New Jersey. Despite being only twenty, Alyn managed to

Alyn McCauley, No. 18 – CHL Player of the Year,
Photograph courtesy of the CHL and Dan Hamilton, Vantage Point Studios

make a big impression at the Leafs' camp. His performance earned him a spot on the roster and an NHL debut.

Despite his jump to the NHL, Alyn did see some ice time on the Leafs' farm team. When the season ended for the Ottawa 67's Alyn packed up and headed for the Rock to join the Leafs' farm team. He caught up with the St. John's Leafs during the playoffs.

It was a tough time to try to blend with a new team but Alyn made a relatively smooth transition to this level of play. The experience helped him to be more comfortable going into the Leafs' training camp. The stint let him get a glimpse of how hard the players work on their physical conditioning.

Being in the NHL was always Alyn's dream but the reality took some adjustment. It is hard to associate yourself with players like Mats Sundin and Felix Potvin but it is important to feel that you belong and can play at the NHL level. He credits these veterans with setting an example. They demonstrate the time, effort and dedication that you have to bring to the game, not just to make it to the NHL but to stay there.

By the spring of his first season with the Leafs Alyn has adjusted to being an NHL player but he still has special moments. Like his first goal or sharing ice with a childhood hero. When the team played the Rangers, Alyn made sure his family was there with a camera. If he was going to play against Wayne Gretzky, he wanted pictures.

Alyn played a defensive role with the team in his first season. In the 1998-99 season he took a more offensive role. Alyn centres the Leaf's second line, a position that will showcase the offensive talent that made him such a promising junior player.

On a Personal Note

When Alyn is not jetting across North America because of the hectic NHL schedule, he likes to relax playing pool with friends. His music of choice is the Tragically Hip. He does not watch a lot of T.V. but he is a movie buff. When he is not training during the summer he likes to hit the golf course. Although he sticks mostly to pasta, chicken and fish during the season, when he gets the chance Alyn likes to snack on chicken fingers and calamari (squid).

Chapter 4
THE WESTERN HOCKEY LEAGUE (WHL)

THE WESTERN HOCKEY LEAGUE (WHL) was formed in 1966 with seven franchises. The original franchises were in Alberta and Saskatchewan. The league grew and in 1976 became international when the Edmonton franchise moved to Portland, Oregon. Three additional teams in Washington made for a solid presence in our southern neighbour. The league now has eighteen teams spread across the four western provinces and two states, divided into three divisions.

The WHL covers a wide geographic region and the majority of the seventy-game schedule is played within the divisions. However, all teams meet each other at least once during the season. This can make for some interesting road trips. To travel from Seattle to Prince George takes eleven hours by road, and these two teams are in the same division.

WEST DIVISION	CENTRAL DIVISION	EAST DIVISION
Kamloops Blazers	Calgary Hitmen	Brandon Wheat Kings
Kelowna Rockets	Kootenay Ice	Moose Jaw Warriors
Portland Winter Hawks	Lethbridge Hurricanes	Prince Albert Raiders
Prince George Cougars	Medicine Hat Tigers	Regina Pats
Seattle Thunderbirds	Red Deer Rebels	Saskatoon Blades
Spokane Chiefs		Swift Current Broncos
Tri-Cities Americans		

- **For an introduction to the cities and the teams see the reference section at the end of the book.**

27

PLAYER IN PROFILE: JOSH HOLDEN

Regina Pats star centre Josh Holden made his hockey debut at age five. Although he was born and raised in Calgary, his family was living in St. Albert during his first hockey season. Josh is the youngest member of the Holden family and the only boy. Twin sisters Michelle and Melinda are big fans of their little brother, although at 6 feet, 180 pounds he is not exactly little.

On the Game

Playing gives Josh a rush of self confidence. It is something he has always loved and excelled at. If he has a bad game he tries to figure out what he can do better. He tries to leave any worries he has about his game in the dressing room. This can be hard to do but it comes with maturity.

On the Position

During his career Josh has logged some time behind the blue line. He played defence for two years when he was ten to twelve years old.

Josh Holden as a younger player
*Photograph courtesy of the
Holden family*

The coach put him back to carry the puck out. He carried it out, then he put it in the net. Josh has no complaints about his time as a defenceman. There was a shortage on the team and it meant he was getting lots of ice time. When he made the move to Peewee he also made the move back to centre.

On the League

Josh was fourteen when he was picked up in the Bantam draft by the Regina Pats. He was also getting some inquiries from NCAA teams. Because he was playing AAA Midget at fifteen, the NCAA teams thought he was older. Josh and father Jody sat down and considered his options. Josh knew a bit about the WHL from guys who had gone to play. He decided that the WHL was a more developmental

Josh Holden, No. 21
Regina Pats
Photograph courtesy of Dan Hamilton, Vantage Point Studios

league than the National Collegiate Athletic Association (NCAA). He packed up and headed for camp when he was sixteen. He was excited to go away and play hockey.

It was a very different game in the WHL: bigger, stronger and faster. Josh says the step from Midget to Major Junior is like the step from Major Junior to the NHL. The lifestyle was pretty demanding and the schedule was a very tough adjustment.

Josh considers himself lucky to have had great billets during his time with the Pats, including his current billet family. At nineteen Josh sees the young couple he lives with more as older siblings than hockey parents. He has been with the couple for a year and a half.

Road Trips

Being a veteran in the league has some advantages. One of those advantages is the three seats at the rear of the bus. Josh shares these posh digs with another player. They alternate sleeping on the seat and the floor. When he started in the league the travel schedule was very tough. By his fourth season, it was no problem.

Josh sleeps a lot during trips. When he is awake he plays cards, watches movies or reads magazines. He has a subscription to *National Geographic* and hopes to do some recreational traveling in the future. If the team loses it means no movies and an early lights out.

Biggest Fans

Josh's parents, Jody and Betsy Holden, try to catch their son's games when road trips swing him through Alberta. With a new CHL team in Calgary the family got to see Josh play in his home town. The Holdens also make the occasional trip to Regina to check out a home game and visit with their son. The team's annual swing down through the United States has also become an annual vacation for the Holdens as they follow the team to Spokane and Tri-Cities.

Josh's family are sensitive to times when he needs extra encouragement. His parents have been known to make the five-hour drive to Swift Current, Saskatchewan. Or the six-hour drive to Saskatoon to watch one game and drive home after a brief visit in the restaurant following the game. Josh really appreciates the boost he gets from his biggest fans.

Quitting? I Don't Think So.

When he was sixteen Josh had a pretty tough year. The team was not doing well. It was his rookie season and he was trying to adjust to the faster, tougher league. Despite the problems Josh wanted to play through it. His goal was to be a career athlete and he was definitely not ready to give up.

Josh credited his father's support with keeping him focused. When it is tough, he recommends trying to get back to the fun. The year did end on a high note when Josh was named the Pats Rookie of the Year.

Second Season

Josh came back at seventeen and had a stellar year. He racked up an impressive 112 points. He led the team in goals, assists and points. Since it was also his draft eligible year it was a good time for a strong performance. It earned him an invitation to the 1995-96 All-Star game.

The All-Star game was not the only big game Josh would be attending. Ranked fourth by Central Scouting, Josh also got an invitation to the 1996 CHL Prospects Challenge game at Maple Leaf Gardens in Toronto. It was a pretty awesome experience for the young player.

Despite having the most shots on net he never managed to get one past the goalie. Josh was playing for Team Orr and admits it was pretty cool having a famous coach. During the game he did glance over his shoulder to catch a glimpse of the famous "Number 4," Bobby Orr.

The game was a great opportunity to meet the other top players. The prospects get to exchange stories and get an idea of what is going on in the other leagues. The guys did get in some recreational activities. They headed down to check out the Hockey Hall of Fame and grabbed dinner at Wayne Gretzky's Restaurant.

Josh may not have put the puck in the net at the Prospects Game but he got the goal that counted for the Pats. During the Playoffs, Josh scored the game winner in quadruple overtime against the Lethbridge Hurricanes. The 3-2 victory ended the longest game in WHL history.

Draft Day

Draft day is a big day for players. The 1996 NHL Entry Draft at the Kiel Centre in St. Louis was Josh's turn to get one step closer to an NHL career. Josh was sharing a room with Daniel Briere at the hotel in St. Louis. His agent represented both players and had made the arrangements. Josh's parents were also there for the big day.

NHL Central Scouting had rated Josh fourth so he was cautiously optimistic about an early pick. He had spoken with the first nine teams in line to select players in the draft the night before. All the teams expressed interest. Josh admits his agent was careful to prepare him for an upset in the draft. Sometimes teams got caught up in drafting a particular position and you went lower than you were projected.

Josh understood that but was getting a little concerned when the first eleven players were selected and he wasn't one of them. Of those eleven early choices seven were defencemen. Vancouver made their selection after a commercial break. It was a pretty exciting moment when they made Josh the twelfth player overall in the 1996 Entry Draft. Josh was happy to be drafted by a Canadian team and one that was so close to his family and friends.

Summer Training

Josh spent some time in the earthquake state during the summer. He did experience a very small quake during his time in L.A. He was not on vacation, but was attending a special development camp put on by his agent. He was once again rooming with Daniel Briere as the two players prepared to make an impression at their respective NHL camps.

Josh's agent likes to get the younger players used to playing with NHLers. Holding these summer development camps helps the guys get in shape and get over the awe factor. Josh is a really social guy and likes meeting other players.

Hockey is hockey wherever you play it but it wouldn't be Tinseltown if you didn't see stars. Academy-award-winning actor Cuba Gooding Jr. stopped by to play a scrimmage game with the players. Ontario native Tom Cruise was also supposed to stop by for a pick up game but never made it. Jerry Brukheimer, producer of the movies *The Rock* and *Con Air*, also stopped by to hang out with the guys.

Going To Camp

After his summer in L.A. Josh packed up and headed for Vancouver's camp. It was a big step. The game was faster and the guys were a lot bigger. Despite the size and speed Josh found it easier to create opportunities. The calibre of players was high and everyone played his position. That made it easier to play.

There is definitely an awe factor to attending a pro camp. At one point Josh found himself sitting in the practice rink's dressing room between Mark Messier and Pavel Bure. He could not believe he was there—where else would Vancouver put their first round draft pick? He was a bit star-struck and sometimes just found himself watching Messier tape his stick or skate around. It is something you have to shake yourself loose from so you can focus on playing.

Josh credits Canuck's Coach Tom Renney with helping him develop. He offered lots of tips but really kept Josh's confidence sky high during the camp and the five exhibition games. Josh got to hit the road with the team; he played in San Jose, Anaheim and Tacoma (against L.A.). It was a pretty amazing opportunity for the young centre.

Josh Holden, No. 21
World Junior Tournament
Photograph courtesy of Dan Hamilton, Vantage Point Studios

Unfortunately, he just missed making the trip to Japan for the start of the season. He signed a contract with the team the day before the trip. The team was leaving for Japan in the afternoon but Josh was boarding a flight back to Regina in the morning. He was being re-assigned back to the Pats. The trip would not have been Josh's first visit to the Land of the Rising Sun. He played in Japan with the Under-18 National Team.

Back In Junior

The Pats were happy to see Josh return. He had definitely been a solid contributor with fifty-three points in thirty games.

The return to junior allowed Josh to play in the WHL All-Star game in Regina. He scored a goal and got two assists at the game. Josh also earned a spot on the National Junior Team.

He was very proud to have been selected to represent Canada. Despite the team's poor performance Josh appreciated the chance to play with some of the best young players in Canada. An avid traveler, Josh also enjoyed getting to see the sights. He remembers that compared to Canadian cities the buildings in Helsinki were very old.

Players and Dream Lines

When it comes to choosing a favourite NHLer Josh split the category and picked two favourites. His favourite current player is Joe Sakic and his favourite retired player is Mario Lemieux. Despite their favourite player status neither made Josh's dream line. Given the opportunity he would centre himself between Phoenix's Jeremy Roenick and the Flyer's Eric Lindros. It is a good thing it is a dream line. Telling the Big E to move over and play wing might not go over well.

Playing In the NHL

Josh may not be playing on his dream line but he is playing against them. Josh started out the 1998-99 season with the AHL's Syracuse Crunch. Early in the season he was called up to play with Vancouver when injuries left holes in the lineup. He has yet to see a significant amount of ice time but playing with the big team gives Josh a chance to learn the NHL game.

On a Personal Note

When he is not on the road or on the ice Josh likes to relax in front of the T.V. He prefers sitcoms like *The Simpsons* and *Seinfeld*. His must-see T.V. is the *Jerry Springer Show*. That will definitely get his mind off the game.

Josh is a fan of the big screen and his most recent favourite is the blockbuster *Titanic*. He also likes to relax with his Sony PlayStation. In the summer he hits the golf course. At the end of his junior career he planned to head to Mexico with a group of players for a well-deserved vacation.

Chapter 5
MAKING AN EDUCATED DECISION

"What you see in an accomplished hockey player is only one dimensional. The most successful are diverse, articulate, intelligent young men with aspirations that go beyond playing professional hockey. Certainly they all have The Dream but they know that to have hockey as the only focus in their life can be a gamble. Sport is such a fragile, fickle business with so many factors beyond their control."

– Jim Donlevy, Education Counsellor, WHL

ANXIOUS TO FOLLOW in the footsteps of top prospects like Giguere, Holden and McCauley? Before you jump into the league it is a good idea to consider your options. There are two main options open to the career-minded young player.

DECISIONS, DECISIONS

Players need to choose carefully. The NCAA and CHL hockey are mutually exclusive choices. The National Collegiate Athletic Association (NCAA) is a volunteer organization that is the supervising body for intercollegiate athletics in the United States. The organization deals with many sports, including football, baseball, basketball and hockey. The NCAA considers Major Junior to be a professional league and will not allow former players into its system.

Under the regulations and standards articulated by the NCAA, young players are offered athletic scholarships to American universities. That means players are older when they move away from home and the game schedule is significantly shorter. The hockey season starts in October and is finished in March.

Major Junior players often attend Canadian Universities when they have finished their junior careers and many play on the varsity teams. Very few players move from the CIAU to the NHL. Most players consider CIAU hockey a great way to play competitive hockey while pursuing their education.

Players who choose the CHL move away from home at a younger age, usually sixteen or seventeen. The schedule in the CHL is very intense with approximately seventy games in the regular season. The season starts in September and ends with the Memorial Cup Tournament in May.

One of the big issues with players and parents is what happens if hockey does not become a career option? Getting a university education seems to offer a safety net for players. It is the unfortunate reality that very few young players have what it takes to make it in the NHL.

THE CANADIAN HOCKEY LEAGUE

With fifty-four teams, the CHL is the largest reservoir of young hockey talent in Canada. While remaining a tough developmental league, the league also recognizes the importance of a solid academic foundation. The league provides financial assistance to allow former players to pursue academic interests when they age out of the league at nineteen years of age or for the few over-age players, twenty years of age.

This chapter looks at the education packages offered by the three CHL leagues. The chapter also highlights some initiatives by teams and the leagues designed to ensure that players are getting an education during their tenure as Major Junior players. The leagues recognize that cautious parents and far-sighted players give serious consideration to educational options when making decisions about which path to take.

EDUCATION SCHOLARSHIP AGREEMENTS

Western Hockey League

During their tenures as players, all education costs are paid by the team. This includes tuition and books for players taking university or college courses. These costs are separate from the package offered at the end of the player's league career and are not deducted from that amount.

Education packages available to players in the WHL have been standardized to prevent teams with larger budgets from benefiting at the expense of the smaller franchises. They cannot offer more lucrative packages. Standardization is enforced by penalties.

The Western Hockey League guarantees the payment of tuition and book expenses to players who go on to a college or university after aging out of the Major Junior system. The agreement provides that for each year played in the league, the player receives the yearly cost of tuition and books applicable to any career development program.

Since players may be in the league for several years the cost of university or community college may have increased dramatically. The escalation of tuition expenses is overcome by indexing the scholarship to reflect actual tuition fees and book expenses when the player finishes hockey and becomes a full-time student. The package is available only to players who do not sign an NHL contract.

Ontario Hockey League

League policy requires that while a player is playing in the OHL all living expenses, tuition and book expenses are paid for by the team whether the player attends high school, college or university.

There is no league policy standardizing the education agreements made between the team and the players for post-hockey education. Different teams have different policies on education packages. The two main options are customized packages, tailored to a particular player, and standardized packages where all the players receive the same education package.

For teams that customize the education packages negotiation starts early as players or their representatives negotiate for the best possible education package. The Plymouth Whalers don't have a standard package. Steven Spott, Assistant Coach of the Plymouth Whalers, indicates that all players get a package but it is completely negotiable with no minimum requirement. The package can only be applied to furthering the player's education.

The Belleville Bulls and Guelph Storm also customize their education packages. The Barrie Colts have a base package that is customized. The Oshawa Generals customize their packages but according to Director of Operations Wayne Daniels, all players receive a contribution towards their future education. The Sudbury Wolves use a sliding scale depending on draft position to determine the education package.

Not all OHL teams have followed this route. The Peterborough Petes adopted a standard non-negotiable package. This break from tradition occurred in the 1992-93 season.

According to GM Jeff Twohey the reasoning behind standardization is to equalize the players. With customization players who are drafted early get big packages while players drafted later may get little or nothing. Twohey recognizes the money won't pay for a player's whole education but believes the package is a fair contribution.

The team holds firm in the face of agent demands for better packages. Twohey sold the players on the package by taking away the uncertainty. Players do not have to be looking over their shoulders wondering how much their teammates are getting. Twohey focuses on the support and guidance that players receive in reassuring parents and attracting players. The Peterborough Pete's position as league champions in 1992-93 demonstrate that their standard package policy is not detracting from the quality of the players.

Quebec Major Junior Hockey League
League policy requires that the team will pay all the costs of education and of academic material while the player is with the team. The league does have a standard education package available to players to allow them to pursue their education when they have completed their time in the league. In 1997-98 the amount allocated was $10,500 for three years for a student.

There are some conditions. The package is only available to players who have played a minimum of two seasons in the QMJHL and one of those years must be the final year of junior eligibility. For the purposes of these criteria, age nineteen is considered to be the last year of eligibility. The player must enroll in a Canadian university within six months of receiving the package.

This league's education package is similar to a scholarship. There is an academic requirement to continue receiving the package. A player must pass seventy-five percent of his courses in each session. The player will receive money twice yearly for three years. The league does not prevent teams from making additional contributions to the education packages of players. The result is a league-wide base amount and customization by team.

MORE THAN MONEY
The leagues go further than a cash payout at the end of the player's career. If the player does not have an academic foundation to build on,

he will not get into a post-secondary institution. Counseling and encouragement are provided as early as possible.

All teams across the league share some common initiatives to help balance school and hockey. The majority of games are scheduled on the weekends. In addition, practices are scheduled so as not to conflict with school attendance. Every year awards are given by the leagues to the top academic players.

Western Hockey League: the Education Counselor

For the Western Hockey League, part of the commitment to education involves the employment of a full-time Education Counselor. Jim Donlevy has occupied this role for the last five years. Donlevy taught at the University of Alberta for over twenty years as well as coaching the Golden Bears football team to two Vanier Cup wins. With respect to his change of sports Donlevy says that athletes are athletes regardless of the sport. They will face the same sorts of pressures and conflicting priorities.

Getting the Job Done

And what does this mean in practical terms? Donlevy's role as Education Counselor has not relegated him to a desk job. Every year he hits the road, traveling to each of the eighteen WHL teams to ensure that academics remain a priority. He tries to meet with players individually during his pilgrimage. In the fall he makes the eight thousand-km trek to visit the Canadian teams and in January he heads south to visit the four American franchises.

This is a big a job for one person. Donlevy has contacts and liaisons in every team in the league who provide local support for the players. If you are wondering how difficult it could be to enroll a player in the nearest high school, you are seriously underestimating the amount of work undertaken by these individuals. A player could be moving to any team in one of four provinces or two states. The academic requirements for graduation and post-secondary education can vary considerably across these seemingly inconsequential borders. It requires careful planning and organization by the teams' education liaisons and the player's hometown educators.

The hockey season can end for a particular team anytime after the playoffs begin. The players usually pack up and head home for a well-deserved rest. Unfortunately they are in the middle of the academic year. The teams coordinate with local high schools to allow the players to transfer back to their hometown high schools to finish the remaining months. Most WHL players are able to graduate with their classmates in their home towns.

Getting an Early Start

Since players are sixteen and often in grade eleven by the time they get into the league how do you ensure they have the right curriculum? By communicating with young players.

In addition to his duties with the teams and WHL players, Donlevy speaks at various Bantam excellence camps throughout Western Canada. He speaks to both players and parents about the importance of education. The Prospects' pamphlet and the paper, *Where Do I go From Here? How to Blend Hockey and Education*, provide practical guidance to parents and players.

The materials provide information on the importance of the core courses such as math, English, science and social studies. It suggests that the player keep up or if possible take a heavy course load or summer courses to be further ahead when he starts playing Major Junior hockey. The materials offer advice for students from grade nine to post-secondary levels.

Dealing With Reality

Donlevy indicated that myth and misinformation are the most dangerous obstacles to a young athlete's academic success. Young players sometimes feel that hockey is everything and that schoolwork can be ignored. This problem is compounded when parents share this delusion.

The unfortunate reality is there are more Major Junior teams than NHL teams and every year there is a "graduating class" of players. This is not true for the NHL where players seem to be having longer careers. Players may finish Major Junior in a year when they do not have the skill set that an NHL team is looking for or the player could be a late bloomer. Donlevy likens strong academic achievement to life insurance. It provides more opportunities to players, just in case.

Donlevy recently sat down with a young player who had "blown off" school. He did not feel that school was important and put minimal effort into academics. This is the most frustrating scenario, where a player achieves below his potential because he does not put any effort into his education

The player had been drafted into the WHL but his team expressed concerns about his academic record. Donlevy sat down with him and designed a program that would provide the core academics. The player buckled down and began doing well.

The informational materials offered by the WHL encourage a player to think about life goals by considering what kind of career he plans to pursue after high school, what he wants to be doing ten years from now, what happens when he finishes playing hockey and what he should be doing to improve his life skills.

Does this mean that players should be doing university degrees during their stint in Major Junior? That is not necessarily a realistic goal.

So are players encouraged to wait until they finish hockey to begin post-secondary education? No.

In the WHL all players, once they have completed high school, are encouraged to enroll in one or two college or university courses during the season. This helps players leaving the league as they are sometimes able to parachute into second or third year of undergraduate programs. Since these courses are fully funded, players can explore their educational interests without incurring any expenses.

The league offers some advice on the most flexible courses. Suggesting English, math, a second language, sociology, psychology or business courses as practical credits to transfer to an academic degree, Donlevy will meet with individual players at their request for career counseling.

Ontario Hockey League: Team Initiatives

The Ontario Hockey League may lack an Education Counselor for the league but individual teams take steps to ensure that their players do well academically. In Detroit (now Plymouth) players are enrolled in one of two private schools and the team imposes a mandatory study hall three times per week. To reach future players the team sends out the best possible spokesmen: current Whalers travel to schools to speak to young people about the importance of academics.

Assistant Coach Steve Spotts, a former Division I player at Colgate College, NY, majored in Education and emphasizes the importance of academics to his players. When they finish high school, players are able to take courses from Michigan University.

Alan Miller, GM of the Guelph Storm, draws a hard line when it comes to education. If you don't attend high school you don't play. This sentiment is echoed by the Oshawa Generals Director of Hockey Operations, Wayne Daniels. If you want to play in Oshawa you go to school. There are two exceptions to this policy, players who are returned from the NHL too late to be enrolled in school and European players who have difficulty with English. The European players are required to take

English Language Studies

Mr. Daniels says that players are not segregated by their academic competence. If players have difficulties the team provides assistance and the goal is still to ensure that all players graduate with a high school diploma. As Mr. Daniels points out, some people, whether they are hockey players or not, have more difficulty with school.

He believes the support and guidance offered by the Generals is first rate. If it takes some players a little longer with some courses then the team will stick it out with them. It's only if they give up and drop out of school that players are sent home.

Like many of the teams, the Belleville Bulls make sure that the numerous road trips do not disrupt the players' education by having mandatory study sessions during trips. The Bulls also provide encouragement in the form of a monthly achievement award of $100 in addition to a yearly award and a team scholarship.

All Peterborough Petes players attend the same high school, Thomas A. Stewart High School. The players have the same homeroom and report to their academic adviser. On a monthly basis reports on each player's attendance, attitude and progress are made to the GM and these reports are forwarded to parents. Team management takes reports from the school very seriously.

Mr. Twohey recounts a problem about three years ago with a rookie player who had a lackadaisical attitude towards attendance. Mr. Twohey recognizes that players have different levels of academic ability and all he requires is a sincere effort. Not attending classes is not a sincere effort. This player continued to be disruptive and to underachieve. He was benched and went home for Christmas with a stern warning. When he returned he did not improve and was sent home. When the player returned next season he buckled down and did better at school.

Quebec Major Junior Hockey League: Language Difficulties

The QMJHL has some additional concerns when it comes to education. Not only are the languages different between the Quebec and Nova Scotia teams (Moncton and Bathurst are in the only officially bilingual province, New Brunswick) but the CEGEP program in Quebec is different from the twelve-grade program in the Maritimes.

The Moncton Wildcats have recently improved their education program, copying the system from the Halifax Mooseheads. To accommodate the different languages and course requirements they created two classes at a local community college where there are two teachers and a number of tutors. The players do all their coursework through correspondence courses. They graduate from wherever the work comes from and all the work is approved by the hometown school.

In Rimouski, players are able to complete courses by correspondence. This allows English-speaking players to keep up with their studies. The Cape Breton Screaming Eagles and the Halifax Mooseheads ensure that players have all the assistance they require by providing tutors.

A PLAYER'S PERSPECTIVE ON EDUCATION: LIFE AFTER HOCKEY

From OHL to NHL to B.A., LL.B and M.H.S.A., Jean Marc MacKenzie has had a lot of initials in his life. During his Major Junior career he made it to the 1985 Memorial Cup Tournament. He got the brass ring in the form of an NHL contract with the Hartford Whalers. Injuries forced him out of the league, but his education and skills earned him an executive position with a major Canadian company.

Making the Decision

When Jean Marc MacKenzie decided to pursue hockey he had to consider his options. With one brother playing NCAA in Ohio and the other brother playing in the QMJHL, he had some personal insight into what the options offered. MacKenzie decided to test his skates and sharpen his skills in the QMJHL. Canadian university would still be available in a few years when he had aged out of the league.

Deciding that Major Junior offered the best hockey development, the youngest member of this hockey family headed for Ontario, a long way from Cape Breton. The decision not to wait for an NCAA scholarship wasn't a decision to exclude education. With a high school principal for a father, this was one hockey player who was sure going to balance academics and hockey.

Going To School

At sixteen, MacKenzie headed for Sault St. Marie to join the Greyhounds. MacKenzie was going into grade eleven. And he was definitely going—attendance at high school was mandatory for players. MacKenzie credits then-General Manager Sam McMaster with the team's strong academic focus. The team monitored players' Christmas and final report cards. A player having difficulty was expected to speak up.

Located in northern Ontario, the Greyhounds had the most travel time in the league. To help travel-worn players the team offered a lot of assistance. This assistance took the form of counselors to help with course selections and tutors to help with the courses.

MacKenzie admits school required self discipline and focus. His marks took a dip during his time in Major Junior. He went from 80-90s to 70-80s. The dip did not keep MacKenzie out of Western. In his final year of Major Junior MacKenzie was traded to the London Knights and picked up half a year's worth of credits towards his B.A.

MacKenzie graduated from high school in his last year with the Soo. Playing hockey had tacked an extra year onto his time in high school but MacKenzie thinks it was a fair trade. And no, he isn't talking about the NHL contract he signed, he is talking about character development and life skills.

Things That Don't Show Up On a Report Card

Major Junior players are role models for young players and celebrities in their communities. This star status brings responsibilities. It means press conferences, volunteer events, and public statements. Players develop people skills and public confidence. Mackenzie jokingly noted that after Major Junior he never needed public speaking classes.

The team had a demanding schedule and players needed to be disciplined and focused. The team fostered a professional mindset—not just on the ice but in the player's interaction with the community. The full resources of the community were available to players and this included interaction with the business community. MacKenzie credits his success as a lawyer and businessman as much to his experiences in Major Junior as he does to his three degrees.

Life After Major Junior

MacKenzie got what every Canadian boy dreams of—an NHL contract. The contract took the form of a two-year plus option deal with the Hartford Whalers. This contract followed on the heels of a great junior season for MacKenzie, a season that saw him tie at third in the league's scoring race. MacKenzie made the move to Binnigham of the AHL to finish out the season.

The next season he was moved to Milwaukee where he played the full season before injuring the crucial ligament in his knee. This sent MacKenzie into rehab but he was ready to start the next season with the Whalers. Unfortunately in a pre-season game against Montreal he once again tore the ligaments in his knee.

It was decision time. MacKenzie was concerned that he would end up riding the buses back in the minors. That was not the future he wanted. With the help of his agent, MacKenzie bought out the rest of his contract and headed for university. He had always been a bit of a club house lawyer so he didn't have to look far for a career choice.

MacKenzie headed home to Nova Scotia to finish his B.A. and then attended Dalhousie Law School to do a combined bachelor of law and Masters in Health Administration. Degrees in hand he headed back to Ontario, but this time to Toronto where he is now employed as Senior Vice President of Medcan. The company helps large corporations and governments restructure their medical benefits packages. MacKenzie handles corporate development and legal affairs for the company. MacKenzie's decision to leave the NHL didn't end his love affair with hockey. For the past ten years he has owned and run a hockey school in Digby, NS, called Scotia Hockey.

A Final Note

MacKenzie's time in Major Junior and the AHL\NHL combined with his responsibilities at the Scotia Hockey School has exposed him to a large number of players. It has been his experience that by the time players hit Major Junior they have their priorities firmly set. Unfortunately, some players are not coming into the league with a well-balanced set of priorities. Parents sometimes encourage their children to chase the Dream and kids buy into the elusive promise of a career in hockey. This creates a mindset in players where hockey is everything.

MacKenzie thinks this is a problem that must be addressed at the earliest stages of the player's development. A balanced set of priorities is something he tries to emphasize at his hockey school. He credits his time in the league as character-building, but admits that you have to bring the right attitude into the league to get the most out of it.

Chapter 6

BEYOND *JERRY MAGUIRE:* A LOOK AT AGENTS

YOUNG PLAYERS making important career decisions are often getting help from agents. So what do these young prospects know about agents? Maybe they saw *Jerry Maguire*—that was the Hollywood version of a player-agent relationship. They may have caught at least part of the high profile Alan Eagleson trials. That was a pretty sobering look at the player-agent relationship. The reality is that most young players and parents know very little about agents.

The relationship between a player and his agent is very important. This chapter provides some basic information about the agenting process in the NHL. It looks at how agents become agents, how the relationship is regulated and what to watch for when dealing with an agent.

It is not unusual for fourteen- or fifteen-year-old players to be approached by agents offering their services. Players admit it is exciting and kind of cool to have an agent. An agent can be an important source of information and guidance for a young player. The quality of the information really depends on two things: the quality of the agent and the quality of the relationship.

An agent with lots of experience may have quality information but if he is unavailable to his client because of other demands on his time, the player loses out. An agent may be enthusiastic and show up for every game but lack the knowledge to guide the player. The ultimate choice is a personal one: a player needs to feel comfortable with the agent he chooses. That comfort level can be increased by making an educated and well-informed decision. A well-informed decision starts with knowing something about agents, who they are and what they do.

You can no longer simply declare yourself an agent and represent NHL players. If you want to be an agent you must be certified by the National Hockey League Players Association (NHLPA).

THE NATIONAL HOCKEY LEAGUE PLAYERS ASSOCIATION (NHLPA)

You may be familiar with the NHLPA because you see their logo on trading cards, hats, T-shirts and other products. Maybe you caught *NHLPA: Be A Player: The Hockey Show* hosted by Sandra Neil and Brett Lindros on TSN. In addition to the licensing work it undertakes, the NHLPA is also the official bargaining agent for all the players in the National Hockey League.

If the NHLPA represents everyone why do you need an agent? The player's agent will represent him in negotiating his agreement with his NHL Club. Only those agents certified by the NHLPA are entitled to represent a player in salary negotiations with an NHL Club.

So what does the NHLPA do for its membership? Like any unionized group the players in the NHL negotiate certain benefits and working conditions. The collective agreement between the league and the NHLPA deals with things like insurance, discipline, pension entitlement, and working conditions. The NHLPA also negotiates the system rights. These rights include club retention rights, free agency, salary arbitrations and the entry level system.

In addition to negotiating and enforcing the collective agreement, the NHLPA represents individual players if they have a grievance. A grievance may concern either the collective agreement or the Player's Contract entered into by the player.

The NHLPA is designed to serve the interests of NHL players. That can mean in addition to the bargaining and licensing work the NHLPA also provides educational material and seminars on topics that would assist its members. An example of these types of undertakings is the NHLPA's response to the growing awareness of the dangerous long-term effects of concussions. The NHLPA has undertaken research and provided information on concussions to its membership.

Not an NHL Player Yet?

The NHLPA is concerned with both current and future members. The Association takes its responsibility to future members very seriously. NHLPA counsel J.P. Barry often receives phone calls, written requests and e-mails from parents and players requesting information about agents, the NHL Entry Draft and the entry level market. The NHLPA employs three full-time lawyers and they are always willing to answer questions from present and future members.

In addition to responding to requests, the NHLPA is trying to get more information out to young players. All the CHL teams are provided with copies of the Agent Directory and representatives of the NHLPA are trying to get out to speak with young players. However, with fifty-four CHL teams and many players already having agents by the time they reach Major Junior it is difficult to speak with everyone.

HOW AGENTS BECOME AGENTS

Agents of NHL players or prospects need to be certified by the NHLPA. The NHLPA introduced a certification program in January, 1996. The new system requires a prospective agent to complete an application form and pay a registration fee. Agents are required to attend an annual NHLPA seminar to ensure that they are aware of all the relevant legal issues when representing players.

The NHLPA stresses the importance of agents educating players about their rights and obligations. An example of the information the NHLPA expect agents to communicate to players is retention rights. Young players are extremely excited about the NHL draft and the prospect of a career in professional hockey. It is still important for players to be fully aware of their rights and how these rights will affect contract negotiations.

Junior players who opt into the Entry Draft, are drafted at eighteen and continue to play junior, can, if they remain unsigned after two years, re-enter the draft at age twenty. A junior player drafted at nineteen can, if he remains unsigned for two years, become an unrestricted free agent. The actual language of the agreement is more technical and looks at birthdates and current teams but a player can easily determine his status by consulting the NHLPA.

Retention rights and the ability to re-enter the draft or become an unrestricted free agent are important. A young player might go from good to great after his draft; re-entering the draft or waiting to become a free agent might be an appropriate decision. An agent should explain all this to his client and help him make informed decisions.

The NHLPA does not guarantee or endorse the agents they register. The decision to sign with an agent is a personal one made by the player, hopefully after careful consideration. The registration process and the new NHLPA regulations governing agent certification are intended to provide some guidance and certain minimum standards in the relationship.

Making the Application

The application to be registered by the NHLPA requires the prospective agent to answer a number of questions. The applicant must provide information on his or her (yes, there are women agents) educational background. The applicant must also answer questions about his or her prior experience in the field.

There is no particular educational or experiential background required by the certification process. The process allows players to check the credentials of prospective agents. Whatever background an agent has, all agents are required to have an understanding of the law relevant to salary negotiation.

Agents are required to be knowledgeable about the NHLPA and the services it provides to players. To carry out salary negotiations agents must be familiar with the relevant provisions of the NHL\NHLPA Collective Bargaining Agreement. The agreement provides certain parameters for salary considerations. Entry level salaries are restricted by Article Nine of the agreement. The restrictions on a rookie's entry salary are based on the player's age and enforced by compensation limits.

Other sections of the agreement deal with veteran players. For example, Group II restricted free agents are entitled to have their salaries settled by binding arbitration. To effectively represent a player the agent must understand the restrictions and mechanisms that guide the arbitration process.

The application for certification requires agents to identify which services they provide for players. In addition to negotiating a Player Contract, many agents offer additional services. Agents may offer estate and tax planning advice; they may provide or arrange for financial planning and investment. An NHL career can be very lucrative but it can also be very short. Careful money management helps protect a player's long-term interests.

With pro hockey becoming more popular, many young stars are entering endorsement contracts or appearing in movies, television or at special events. Agents can offer assistance in negotiating these opportunities.

Agents may approach players as young as fourteen and fifteen. Since these players are years away from financial concerns an agent can play a different role, acting as a resource for players or helping the player and his family make decisions about choosing a league. Agents are also helping players select skills and conditioning programs.

The information obtained by the certification process is available to players who are trying to select an agent and want to check the agent's credentials. The NHLPA recommends that players always check to ensure that an agent is certified by the NHLPA.

The Regulations

The new certification requirement is part of a new system, the NHLPA Regulations Governing Agent Certification. The regulations bind all the agents certified by the NHLPA. The regulations set standards of conduct for agents in the representation of players during contract negotiation.

The regulations provide that the agents must be certified and give the grounds for denial of certification. In the section that sets the standard of conduct for an agent there is a list of prohibited types of conduct. In addition, the regulations allow players to terminate an agent's representation with fifteen days' notice. Another important provision in the regulations is a mechanism for players and agents to resolve disputes through binding arbitration.

Standard Player-Agent Agreement

The regulations also govern the agreement entered into between the player and the agent. The regulations provide that agents must enter into a Standard Player-Agent Contract (SPAC) and a copy must be filed with the NHLPA. The NHLPA recognizes that players may enter into other contracts for additional services. They require copies of any additional contracts.

The Standard Player-Agent Contract requires the agent to comply with the regulations. The agreement contains provisions relating to the agent's fees and expenses. The formula for the calculation of fees must be attached as a schedule to the agreement. Players need to know what they will be paying for and how, whether by a percentage of earnings or a flat rate.

The NHLPA can provide a current Standard Player-Agent Contract to players who want to compare the contract to what they are signing with their agent. If you are concerned about what you are signing—do the research.

A TYPICAL AGENT

It is difficult to describe a typical agent. In 1998 approximately 250 agents were registered by the NHLPA. Of those, 115 were American-based. Some agents are with large companies that make a full-time business of representing sports figures. Other agents work part time in the field representing one or two clients.

The occupational background is mixed. Agents registered with the NHLPA include former players, lawyers, engineers, athletic therapists, and businessmen. Many of the agents are lawyers, but sports law is a specialized field and a law degree is no guarantee of expertise. There is no profile that adequately describes the typical agent. This variety means that players have a lot to choose from when it comes to selecting an agent who meets their needs.

You're It Kid, the Next Big Thing

You are hanging out with your friends, playing video games, and the phone rings; it is your agent. Pretty impressive. When you are thirteen or fourteen it is pretty exciting to have an agent. It has a big coolness factor.

One player admitted it was fun having an agent who took him out to dinner or to hockey games. Most players realize that some agents are all flattery. They talk about how talented you are, how far you will go. It may be nice to hear but you have to be careful not to let your ego make the decision about which agent you will choose to represent your interests.

Too Many Agents, Too Little Time

Most top players have an agent when they are quite young. Getting an agent can be a very annoying process. The parents of one first round prospect were forced to unplug the phone when agents kept calling to offer their services. This is a very familiar story throughout the league as increased competition and high salaries make talented young players hot properties. It is not unusual for agents to approach parents, coaches and players to offer their services.

Players do not have to choose from the agents knocking on their door. You do not take the first car a dealer shoves in front of you. Why should you choose the first agent to show up on your doorstep? You can shop around.

The NHLPA publishes an Agents' Directory which lists all the registered agents. The Directory provides information on the background and services offered. Players can contact other agents, ask some questions, get a feel for what is available. This process can help players get a clearer picture of their own abilities and what agents offer.

Judging Agents

Players and parents admit it is sometimes difficult to judge agents. When you are thirteen or fourteen it is just exciting; when you turn eighteen and face the Entry Draft it is serious business. One player confessed that at eighteen he has already changed agents. His recommendation is not to sign anything until you know what you are doing. Changing agents is relatively common and that means the proposals and pressure keep coming even after you have selected an agent.

Players tend to have different criteria when it comes to selecting an agent. One player chose a young agent who was just starting out. The player, a second round draft pick, felt that the agent was competent and would have time to focus on his needs and interests.

Another player, also a top pick, went with a veteran agent who had a large client base and lots of experience in the field. The player spoke to several of those clients before making his decision. The agent is part of a big firm that also offers specialized player training and conditioning. Both players are satisfied with their choices.

The best choice of agent may depend on the player's qualities. A high-profile draft prospect may get more attention even from a busier agent whereas a borderline player may get lost in the shuffle. When you hire an agent you are hiring someone to provide guidance and assistance. Know what services your agent promised to provide and expect to get those services. Being an agent is not volunteer work; it can be lucrative. Make sure you get what you will pay for.

Young players often forget that the decisions that are being made are *their* decisions. An agent should provide advice and expertise but ultimately it is the player's call. You will live with the results of the choices that are being made so it is important to make decisions carefully.

GETTING SOME HELP

Trying to make good decisions can be difficult. Most players admit that they are not familiar with the business side of hockey. Often, players want to focus on their game and getting a shot at the NHL. However, poor business decisions can leave a player broke and bitter even after a successful career. Mismanagement early in a career may leave a player sitting on the sidelines while other young athletes get opportunities.

Players should always ensure that they read contracts carefully. Any document that affects your rights and obligations should be reviewed. That includes documents like the NHL\NHLPA collective agreement, the team's rules, and the regulations governing agents. The language can be technical and confusing. If you do not understand ask for an explanation. You can ask your agent or the NHLPA for information.

The NHLPA is always ready to answer questions from its membership. NHLPA counsel J.P. Barry also recommends *An Athlete's Guide To Agents* by Robert H. Ruxin (The Stephen Greene Press, 1989). The book does deal with NCAA eligibility issues and other sports but it also contains some helpful tips on dealing with agents.

Other resources are available to players and parents to help them deal with these difficult decisions. One way to deal with the legal language is to speak with a lawyer. Not all lawyers are sports lawyers but having a lawyer go through an agent's proposal or contract can provide a better explanation of the terms and the legalities. Even if the player has already signed on the dotted line you may want a second opinion.

Just because something looks very official does not mean that it is legally binding on the player. Anyone with a computer and a dictionary can make documents look good. Some players admit that they just go ahead and sign documents. It is never a good idea to sign an agreement you have not reviewed and do not understand, whether that agreement is your contract with your major junior team, your education package, your agent's contract or your NHL contract.

If you are at the stage where money is an issue, you may want to talk to investment counselors or financial advisors. It is important for players to understand where their money goes.

SHOW ME THE MONEY

Unfortunately, not everyone can make a living doing something he loves. NHL hockey players can make a good living at the game. Everybody knows about the multi-million dollar deals star players are making but what does the average player make? What can a middle of the pack rookie expect in his first season? As players get closer to the dream of playing in the NHL these questions are suddenly more important.

The NHL\NHLPA collective agreement has compensation limits for rookies. The compensation limits restrict the salary and signing bonuses but allow plenty of room for performance bonuses. These bonuses can be a tremendous boost to the player's total income. New York Islander Bryan Berard (a former Detroit Whaler) got a $600,000 bonus for winning the Calder Cup. Bruins rookie Sergei Samsonov has performance bonuses that could net him an extra million in 1998-99.

NHL money is paid only to NHL players. Most young players have two-way contracts. This means they have an AHL or IHL and an NHL salary. Players are paid according to which league they are assigned to by the NHL team holding the player's rights. Players in a hurry to spend their lucrative incomes should make sure that they are actually earning it.

With dozens of young players signing NHL contracts every year players may wonder how you determine the appropriate salary. This is not as tough as it sounds—check the market. There is an entry level market for NHL players. The NHLPA keeps data on all the contracts that are being signed and this information provides a market. Players price their services according to the going rate for someone with their qualities. To get an idea of how you rate, you can get information from the NHLPA on players with similar characteristics.

For example, Player X is a third round draft choice, an offensive defenceman. He has 25 assists and 13 goals, and he also accumulated 205 penalty minutes. The NHLPA can pull information about other rookie defenceman with similar characteristics who recently signed an NHL contract.

Obviously, determining a player's salary is not an exact science. Negotiation and the structuring of signing and performance bonuses are important parts of the agent's job. It is important to have realistic expectations when it comes to signing a contract. A bit of research about the market will help a player feel more comfortable when he makes a decision to accept a club's offer.

UP CLOSE AND PERSONAL: A LOOK AT SOME AGENTS

Ever wonder what agents actually do? Why they got into the industry? Patrick Morris is an eleven-year veteran of the business. He joined an established company with a large client base. Don Horne became a full-time agent about five years ago and the first of his young prospects are starting their professional hockey careers now. These two agents share some information about their backgrounds, their jobs and their views on the industry.

Patrick J. Morris, Newport Sports Management Inc.

Morris started his career because of an interest in the sport. Like so many young Canadians, Morris was a player. He played at the highest level throughout his teens and went on to play varsity. He was an enthusiastic player but the NHL was not in his future. After being part of the Ontario Championship-winning Toronto Varsity Blues he moved to a slower game—recreational/intramural hockey at Queen's Law School.

Hockey remained a driving force in his life. But how did he translate that into a career? Well, it all started when he arranged for a guest speaker as part of his involvement with the Entertainment Law Division at Queen's Law School. The guest speaker was Don Meehan, a prominent Toronto sports agent. A career was sparked, at least as soon as Morris finished law school, articled for a year and managed to convince Meehan that there was room for an enthusiastic young associate.

Morris joined Newport Sports in October, 1986. Now that he was in, he needed to show that he could get the job done. He focused on building a practice serving young Ontario players. The players would be recruited at fifteen or sixteen when they were just entering OHL eligibility. Morris would provide the players and their parents with information about the options open to young players. The two main options for the career-minded young player are OHL and NCAA.

With a consistent recruitment practice Morris was able to enter the 1991 season representing a talented group of OHL players. Todd Harvey, Ethan Moreau, Chris Gratton, Larry Courville, Todd Bertuzzi, Jamie Allison, Jamie Rivers, Kevin Brown, Jason Arnott, Ryan Sittler, Jamie Storr and Chris Pronger were on the roster. Well, we know where these guys ended up. So what was Morris doing for these guys back in their Major Junior days?

When it comes to young players Morris' main role is to be a source of professional advice and information. Recognizing that the decision about which route to take is a personal one, Morris helps players and parents understand and evaluate the OHL and the NCAA route. Is that all he does? Well not exactly; these fledgling players aren't signing big NHL contracts (yet) but they do need to negotiate an education package with their OHL team and if things go well, prepare for the NHL Entry Draft.

Morris focuses on more than career choices and contracts. In the early stages of their careers players are learning and improving. Morris helps by providing assistance in selecting appropriate developmental options including power skating and conditioning programs.

Does this mean that you have to be a hot draft prospect to need an agent? You should probably ask Rob Zamuner, except he is busy playing his sixth NHL season in sunny Tampa Bay. Zamuner was Morris' first client. He was never drafted into junior but he was hard-working and motivated and he just kept grinding until he got picked up by the New York Rangers. The hard work paid off; this player got a spot on the 1998 Olympic team.

Don Horne, Sports Management International Limited

Don Horne started out in sports and event marketing and met a number of people involved in the sports industry. He decided he was interested in becoming an agent. Decision made, he did what any good marketer does—research.

He talked to some General Managers and he sat down and had a long chat with Glenn Healy, an NHL veteran, about his experiences with agents. When he began his practice there were no other agents in Nova Scotia. Horne recognized the talent coming out of the Atlantic provinces and concentrated on local players.

For those interested in joining what is a rapidly growing field Horne has a word of caution. There is significant startup time. You approach players when they are quite young and it is a number of years before agents receive any financial benefit.

If you are wondering how young the players are, Horne says that even fourteen is becoming too late to contact players. It is a competitive industry that requires patience and diligence. Horne's efforts have paid off as his young players are beginning their professional careers. Colin White, a second-round pick for New Jersey in the 1995 draft, signed with the club.

It is difficult approaching players who are so young. After identifying prospects he usually contacts the parents and coach of the player first. He admits it is critical to have a good relationship with the players because as they get older they will be making their own decisions.

He doesn't believe in formal contracts with young players. If he fulfills his end of the deal he expects loyalty from the player. This doesn't always happen; some young players go for agents from bigger firms in bigger centres like New York and Beverly Hills. Part of that phenomenon is the perception that bigger is better.

So what does Horne do for his players? The biggest service he provides is acting as a source of correct, current and objective information. Providing information allows parents and players to make informed decisions. Hockey expects sixteen-year-olds to make decisions that would be tough for forty-year-olds. The QMJHL can be a tough league for young anglo players because of the language and cultural differences. Horne tries to prepare his players and help them stay positive.

Another service this agent provides is a three-month conditioning program. The program started three years ago and runs during the summer months. There are three on-ice sessions per week, no scrimmages, just skills development, and three off-ice conditioning sessions.

The program is small with only twenty-five players. It requires an extraordinary amount of commitment from players, but to realize their great expectations players need to demonstrate that level of commitment. Horne states that talent is nice but you have to have work ethic—real superstars have talent and work ethic. Some players take a long time to truly figure it out and do what is necessary.

So what else does the job entail? Horne spends a lot of time on the road. He visits existing clients and checks out new prospects. There is more to these visits than just checking on the player. Horne also spends some time with the coach, general manager and the parents.

When it comes to identifying potential clients Horne keeps in close contact with the scouting fraternity, and attends AAA Bantam and Midget games. For older players Horne negotiates contracts. His job doesn't end there; he also assists with financial planning and ensures contract enforcement.

If this agent has some advice for players when it comes to dealing with agents it is this: take your time. Young players find it exciting to sign with an agent and they sometimes make quick decisions. Take time to get to know the agents.

See what the agent does over a period of time before you commit to the relationship. Players should also do some research. Talk to other players, to parents and coaches. The player-agent relationship is an important one and players should make an informed long-term commitment.

Chapter 7
AN HONEST ASSESSMENT: DO YOU HAVE WHAT IT TAKES?

MANY PLAYERS dream of making hockey their profession. Unfortunately, few have the talent, the size and the work ethic to make that dream come true. If you have decided to pursue hockey you need to make a careful assessment of what you bring to the game and then be prepared to work hard.

Players at the CHL level are all "good." They have to be to make the team. Players that want to go beyond that level have to be exceptional. The player must have raw talent, meet the physical requirements of a demanding sport and have a strong work ethic.

To play in this highly competitive league a player must be talented; but talent is an elusive concept. People talk about "hockey sense" or a "feel for the game." Scouts like to think that they know it when they see it but every club has top picks that do not make it. Perhaps the most measurable talent is offensive ability. You can check the stats; a player with lots of points is good offensively.

Other talents can be more difficult to assess. Some very successful players are role players. They are defensive forwards or stay-at-home defencemen. At the end of the year they have points in the single digits but they have done their jobs. One young player was upset at a low points tally but logged most of his ice time on penalty killing. Everyone wants to score but those statistics do not define talent.

Understanding your strengths and defining your role is something that a player discovers in the process. Good coaching can be a big factor in this learning process. As players play for more competitive teams they must learn to define their roles more precisely. Experience and the willingness to learn are key components to realizing on that talent.

Talent is critical but it is not the only criterion for a prospect. A small talented player or a lazy talented player might find himself sidelined at this level. This chapter looks at some of the criteria that all players will be assessed against.

The first segment looks at the physical requirements of hockey, the height and weight a player is expected to bring to the game. The final segment provides some insight into what coaches in the CHL are looking for in players.

BIGGER, BETTER, FASTER, STRONGER: THE PHYSICAL ELEMENT

When you talk about playing in the big leagues you can stress BIG, as in the size of the participants. In 1997-98 the average height of players in the NHL was 6'1" and the average weight was two hundred pounds. New players entering the league are being measured by that yardstick. It can be a lot to measure up to, especially for young players.

Players must be eighteen years of age to be eligible for the NHL Entry Draft. Many young players are still growing at that age. Some may have sprouted up to impressive heights but lack the muscle mass of their older counterparts. This segment looks at the importance of size, the persistence of smaller players and the reality of the "filling out" process.

The Scouts Speak

How important is size in the NHL? According to the scouts it is pretty important. Former New York Islanders scout Harry Boyd remembers that Al Arbour always use to say, "It's all right if you miss a small player with talent but do not miss a big guy with talent."

The Islanders have always had a big team and Boyd admits that in today's NHL you really have to. You can afford to have a few small players on the team but you cannot send a small team against a really big team. Even back then, the Philadelphia Flyers were a big team and you needed size to compete.

In the late 1970s the Islanders had a great checking team but they needed some goals. They took a chance on a smallish player named Mike Bossy. Bossy had a ten-year career with the Islanders that included four Stanley Cup victories. Not bad for a player who is considered small by NHL standards.

Boyd notes that smaller players need to be stronger and feistier. They have to be very strong on their skates, and have enough talent to make a team overlook their lack of height. Even talented players can be overlooked if a team already has a couple of smaller players.

Former Toronto Maple Leafs' Scouting Coordinator Dan Marr agrees that size is important. If he is given a choice between a big player and a small player of similar skill he will pick the bigger guy. There is room for smaller players but they need to be exceptional and they need to have good trunk strength.

MEASURING UP: SMALL GUYS WITH BIG DREAMS

The reality is if you are small it is going to be an uphill battle. Before you throw in the towel and give up your hockey dreams take a look at the league. The small players are there, not in abundance, but definitely making a big impression. At 5'6" Calgary Flame's Theo Fleury proves that with every goal he scores.

A Player's Perspective On Size: Derrick Walser, Rimouski Oceanic

Derrick Walser grew up wanting to be a hockey player. This Nova Scotia native earned himself a spot in the QMJHL and looked as if he was on his way to realizing that dream. Unfortunately, according to the NHL yardstick he doesn't quite measure up.

It is hard to think that a few inches could stand between Derrick and an NHL career. At 5'10 1/2" Derrick is two and one half inches shy of the NHL average of 6'1". Derrick admits that it is very frustrating to be constantly judged on the inches he is missing instead of the 5'10 1/2" and 198 pounds that he brings to the game.

Derrick Walser, No. 91
Rimouski Oceanic
Photograph courtesy of the Walser family

Derrick may not have the extra couple of inches but he has the talent. He finished fourth in scoring at the end of the 1996-97 season and earned himself a spot on the QMJHL first all star team. Eighty-three points in sixty-eight games is impressive for a forward; it is exceptional for a defenceman. If you are worried that as a smaller guy Derrick does not have the durability to play, a sixty-eight-game regular season puts that worry to rest.

The 1996-97 season was a strong one for the young defenceman and he admits he had hopes of being selected in the June NHL Draft. Unfortunately, he was passed over in the 1997 Entry Draft. You have to accept that if you are a small player you might not be drafted. This does not mean that Derrick is giving up his goal of playing in the NHL. He is more determined than ever to prove that there is room in the league for smaller players.

A lot of players get a shot at the NHL without being drafted. Derrick knows that he has to get an invite to a camp and make an impression. The invite came quickly for Derrick. Montreal Head Coach Alain Vigneault called the day after the draft with an invitation to camp.

Derrick sees the league getting bigger and admits that big teams take up more space on the ice. Taller players can take longer strides, cover the ice surface more effectively. Despite those advantages, bigger is not always better. The drive for size that might soon make the NHL look like the NBA does not mean that smaller players are out in the cold.

Being smaller means being tougher, not just physically tougher but mentally tough. Derrick works out. He knows he has to be in great shape and strong. You can be a small guy but you still have to make a big impression on the ice. Derrick stays focused on his game and his belief that he can make it even when he is passed over by scouts.

Derrick cites Calgary Flame's Theo Fleury as an example of a small guy making a big impression. At only 5'6" Fleury is a

Derrick Walser
Photograph courtesy of the Walser family

physical player who hits like a big guy. Defenceman Darius Kasparaitis at 5'10" managed to bring down Philadelphia's big gun 6'4" Eric Lindros. A small player has got to be tough, he has to go to the corner every time. Derrick feels that smaller players bring a lot of character and heart to the game. They are fighting the odds to earn a spot and that translates to work ethic.

With a record-setting forty-one goals in the 1997-98 season Derrick didn't let his disappointment over not being drafted impact his performance. Instead, he was even more motivated to prove that he had what it took to play in the NHL. He won't be the only defenceman under six feet in the NHL when he does make it. Players like Phil Housley (5'10"), Brian Leetch (5'11"), Ray Bourque (5'11"), and Don Sweeney (5'10") prove that size is not everything even behind the blue line.

Being smaller can be frustrating for young players. Derrick would like to see size ranked instead of being made an exclusive measure of talent. That might not be a bad idea. The NHL is desperately trying to figure out why game scores have gone down. Maybe more emphasis on selecting and developing high scorers instead of going for size would increase the number of goals being scored in the league and raise the excitement level of the game.

Derrick finished his Major Junior career with CHL Defenceman of the Year honours but no draft interest. That didn't mean no interest. Derrick had a number of invites to NHL camps. He decided to attend the Calgary Flames training camp and ended up signing a three-year contract with the team and headed to New Brunswick to play for the Saint John Flames.

STRONGER PLAYERS: A CAUTION ON WEIGHT LIFTING

Players who want a professional career must be professional about their conditioning and training. For most players weight training forms a part of that commitment. In a later chapter this book takes a closer look at the commitment to exercise and nutrition that players make. This segment looks at a player's desire to be bigger.

Even when players have sprouted up to impressive heights they may be on the slim side. Most players realize that "filling out" is a natural growth process. Some players try to get a jump on nature by intense weight training.

Early weight lifting can be ineffective at best and detrimental at worst, to the player's development. According to Dr. Ron Olson, M.D., C.C.F.P., Dip. Sport Med. and team doctor for the CIAU Dalhousie Tigers and St. Mary's Huskies, strength gains have more to do with age than with weight lifting. He indicates that a thirteen-year-old player who does not lift weights is almost always stronger than a twelve-year-old who does.

Even the difference between a thirteen-year-old who lifts weights and one who does not is small compared to the growth variable among thirteen-year-olds. At young ages, Dr. Olson recommends that players focus on developing their skills, not their biceps.

The reason that weight lifting can be detrimental for very young players is that young players often do not use proper techniques when they lift weights. Improper technique can result in strains and injury to growing bodies. Also, because young players are still growing their growth plates are not fully developed and are more vulnerable to injury. Players should speak with their doctors about when weight training is appropriate.

Sometimes gaining weight is not the goal. Players are expected to be in top physical condition. A player's percentage body fat is a better indication of conditioning than the numbers on the scale. Sarnia Sting goaltender Pat DesRochers had to drop twenty pounds when he returned to camp after the summer.

At 6'3" Patrick could easily carry an extra twenty pounds but as an elite athlete and NHL prospect Pat needed to be in top physical condition. No one made a big deal about the extra weight. It came off pretty easily once Pat got into the routine of practices and games. The team provided guidance about nutrition and conditioning and Patrick had assistance from the team's trainer.

Patrick offers some very practical advice to young players. Do not worry about it. Good eating habits and regular exercise are always important but do not be obsessed with your weight or your measurements. Focus on having fun and enjoying the game. As you get older you will play in more competitive leagues and your conditioning and strength training will increase.

This sentiment is echoed by Kamloops Blazers winger Steve Gainey. He knows that he will have to gain muscle mass to play in the NHL. Healthy eating and regular exercise are important but he knows that maturity will be a big part of the filling-out process. There can be huge differences in muscle mass between a player at twenty-four years old and the same player at sixteen. Scouts and GMs allow for this growth when they select young players.

A VIEW FROM THE BENCH: LET ME SEE YOU WORK

You probably think that different coaches want different things from players. Three coaches found some common ground in what they want from players. Tom Renney (Kamloops Blazers and Vancouver Canucks), Real Paiement (Moncton Wildcats and National Junior Team) and Parry Shockey (Regina Pats) offer some insight into what it takes to make their rosters. Work . . . hard work . . . consistent, honest hard work.

Getting a Reputation With Renney

If you want a good reputation with Tom Renney you have to be a self-starter. You have to be a player who can get himself going and keep himself going through a long and demanding season. A player has to get up for the fiftieth game with the same heart and intensity as the first game.

You have to be mentally and emotionally tough to adjust to all the changes and pressures that competitive hockey can bring. Some changes a player may face include new positions, new lines and even new teams. It can be difficult to deal with these types of changes. The quality of a player's game can fluctuate and the player has to be prepared to be benched if that becomes necessary until the problems can be solved.

No matter how much you prepare, hockey in final analysis is a spontaneous game. There is no way to be one hundred percent accurate in predicting the actions of the other team or even your own. Renney likes to see a responsive, resourceful player, one who is ingenious and creative in the way he deals with things.

Hockey is a team sport and Renney wants team players. A player must be willing to do what is best for the team, which may mean changing positions, lines or the way he plays. If your best for the team is a grinding role position and not star centre, you work hard in that position. A good player identifies with the team and is committed to doing his best for the team.

Pleasing Paiement

Paiement looks for honesty, and this means honesty in effort. He wants a player who gives an honest effort all the time at every task. He also needs players to be accountable and accept responsibility. Character is important, but what does it mean? To Paiement it means showing up for every game and playing the best you can. It means knowing he can count on the player.

Impressing Shockey

Parry Shockey recognizes that players need to have a constant work ethic. There are sacrifices that go with playing in the league.

When twenty-year-old players head home for their ten o'clock curfew, that's discipline. These players have a high profile in their communities and that's a responsibility. Their actions are a reflection on the team and they are required to behave with a level of professionalism that can be pretty surprising in someone so young.

As a parent of two hockey players, Shockey has had some experience with the system. His son Jonathan played Major Junior and his younger son was an avid player until a congenital cartilage problem with his knees forced him out of the game. Jonathan spent three years in the WHL, playing with Tri-city, Swift Current and Spokane.

Shockey recognizes that it takes more than talent. It takes work ethic and commitment to carry a player through the long season. If a player has an ability level of five or six (out of ten) and a work ethic of nine he can make a place for himself. Hard work and commitment will win games. For Shockey the biggest enemy of players is being "good;" you need players who are good but want to be great.

Chapter 8
GETTING A SPOT ON THE ROSTER

THINK YOU ARE UP to the challenge of Canada's elite junior league? Then it's time to learn how a player are gets his name on the roster. Making a big impression at training camp is very important but getting an invitation to camp is the critical first step.

GETTING IN: MAKING THE ROSTER

With fifty-four teams scheduled to play in the 1999-2000 season you are probably wondering, how hard can it be to make a team? Drop by a training camp and you will find out it is pretty hard. With fifty to sixty players vying for twenty-four spots on the roster it is a very competitive process.

THE DRAFT

Despite the number of teams in the league there are more prospects than roster spots. Players who want to play in this league have to make the cut. Like the NHL, the OHL, QMJHL and the WHL select players by way of an Entry Draft.

Each of the three leagues holds a draft for players in its geographic region. Players from Prince Edward Island and Newfoundland, the only two provinces without teams, are eligible to play anywhere in the CHL. As Steve Gainey demonstrates, these boundaries can be crossed when a league is willing to waive rights to a player.

The WHL holds a Bantam draft but players are not eligible to play until the year of their sixteenth birthday. The QMJHL has a Midget Draft and also drafts fifteen-year-olds. In the OHL Priority Draft players are often drafted at sixteen or seventeen from junior teams. "Underage" (fifteen-year-old) players are allowed to be drafted in the first three rounds of the OHL draft. The drafts are all held in the spring.

GETTING DRAFTED; OPPORTUNITY KNOCKS: PLAYERS' PERSPECTIVES

Draft day is always a big day for young players. Each of the three leagues covers a number of cities so players have no way of knowing which team, if any, will draft them. Some players share their experience with the CHL draft.

Dylan Gyori, Tri City Americans

Dylan Gyori definitely wanted to play in the WHL. It was a developmental league that offered the best chance of realizing his dream to play in the NHL. Prior to the draft Dylan spoke to three teams that expressed an interest in the young forward.

Despite these meetings, draft day was a surprise for the prospect. The Tri-City Americans stepped forward to select him in the draft. Dylan had no idea that the team was even interested until it took him in the second round, tenty-eighth overall in the WHL Draft. Dylan found out about his selection when the team called to let him know. In the WHL players often hear about their selection through a phone call or a letter from their new team.

Washington state was a long way from Red Deer, Alberta but Dylan had no complaints. He had been drafted and that was an important step forward in his career goal. Geographic distance and lack of choice did not matter. Dylan wanted the chance to prove himself in the WHL and Tri-City would provide that opportunity.

Dylan recognizes that the drafting process is important. It keeps any one team from becoming too stacked in talent. Drafted at fifteen, Dylan had a year to prepare himself for the move, a move that was still dependent on a strong performance at camp. The draft gets you an audition; you have to earn the right to stay.

Alex Johnstone, Halifax Mooseheads

Alex Johnstone decided to give the QMJHL Draft a try when he traveled with his midget team to a tournament in Quebec and saw the level of skill. He knew that at the Major Junior level it would be elite players. Fortunately, Alex was having a great year. His team went to the Air Canada Cup and he was getting lots of ice time. All the exposure paid off and as the draft approached teams were expressing interest in the young defenceman

Some of the cities in the QMJHL do not have English schools. Alex knew he would have a difficult time with correspondence courses. He and his agent wrote to the teams which could not offer English-speaking schools explaining Alex's preference not to be selected. A number of QMJHL teams do have accessible English schools so there were still a number of options open when it came to the draft. Alex spoke to a number of teams before the draft but he really didn't know where he might end up.

When the day of the draft came around, Alex went fishing. Unwilling to sit by the phone, he went to a fish camp with his dad for three days. On the way home from the camp Alex picked up a paper at the corner store and found out that he had been drafted by Halifax. It was a big surprise; the team had not seemed interested but had selected Alex in the eighth round. If he could earn a spot on their lineup Alex would be playing in his home town.

Patrick DesRochers, Sarnia Sting

The OHL patterns its draft after the NHL. The draft is held at Maple Leaf Gardens and the players come down to the podium to collect their jerseys when their names are called. Patrick DesRochers was one of those players. In 1995, the Sarnia Sting stepped up to claim the underage netminder eighth overall.

Since most players are drafted at sixteen or seventeen, Pat was not really thinking about the draft when he started the season that year. It became apparent by mid-season that some of the teams were thinking of him.

In the days leading up to the draft Pat did a number of interviews with teams. He asked questions about the city and his prospective role on the team. Sarnia told him something he was happy to hear: their goalie was nineteen and they were looking for a young prospect to develop. Pat had a pretty good idea that Sarnia would be selecting him in the draft.

Patrick admits that the draft is exciting but cautions against taking such early assessments too seriously. Drafting is not life or death. The player still has to go to camp and make a good impression. With fifty players on the protected list you still need to work hard to make the team.

NOT GETTING DRAFTED: IT AIN'T OVER YET

Getting drafted is a big deal and not getting drafted is a big disappointment but it doesn't mean the end of the Dream. Every year players are invited to attend training camps and try out for a spot on the team. Every year these "walk-ons" make spots for themselves in this elite league.

A Player's Perspective: *Josh Dill, Cape Breton Screaming Eagles*

Like all young players Josh Dill had hopes of being drafted. He had hopes when he was fifteen and again when he was sixteen. There was a considerable amount of interest from a number of teams but Josh was passed over in the drafts. Despite generating impressive stats on the ice Josh has one stat he can not escape; he is a small player in a league that keeps getting bigger.

Some of the teams told Josh that his smaller size kept him off their draft lists. Although he appreciated their honesty Josh was disappointed and frustrated. He loved the game and was good at it; he just needed the opportunity to prove it.

The opportunity finally came when the Granby Predateurs (now the Cape Breton Screaming Eagles) gave the young forward an invitation to camp. Unfortunately, a car accident kept Josh off the ice that fall. He knew that even if he managed to make the team he wouldn't get much ice time so he decided to return home and give his body some time to recover. The next year Dill returned to camp healthy and anxious to carve out a spot for himself. Before camp, he checked the team's draft prospects and current roster to assess the talent base for his position.

It would be difficult for Josh to make the team. As a smallish walk-on he had a lot to prove. He also knew that if he didn't at least try he would be kicking himself for the rest of his life. He came into camp with a mission. He was on the ice two or three times a day. He had blisters on his feet because his equipment was not fully dried, but he wouldn't give up. Every shift he played hard and he knew he was playing well.

Josh's commitment paid off because when the final cuts were made, he was still there. Despite not getting drafted he had a spot on the team and a

Josh Dill, No. 24
Cape Breton Screaming Eagles
Photograph courtesy of the Cape Breton Screaming Eagles

chance to play in Canada's elite junior league. Half-way through his first full season Josh saw regular ice time and hovered around sixth on his team in scoring.

Steve Gainey, Kamloops Blazers

Steve Gainey did not know much about the Major Junior system when he was growing up. While he was living in Minnesota, Steve played high school hockey but when his family moved to Dallas it created problems for Steve's hockey plans. Although NHL hockey was moving to the Lone Star State there was not really a developmental minor league system.

Steve decided to move north. He went to play with St. Andrew's High School in Toronto. Despite being underage Steve decided to put his name in for the OHL's Entry Draft. He was passed over in the OHL Draft but he was generating some interest in the west. The WHL drafts younger players and the Kamloops Blazers were interested in the young winger.

Unfortunately, Steve was a bit tied up. As an American player he should have been able to go into any league but he had put his name into the OHL Draft. To complicate matters even further, Steve was born in Quebec.

All the OHL teams had to release their rights to Steve before he could head west. The teams were not keen on an already strong Blazers getting rights to the winger even though they had failed to draft him. They finally agreed to release Steve's rights to the Calgary Hitmen. Those rights were promptly traded to Kamloops and Steve joined his new team.

CHL TRAINING CAMPS: GETTING IN THE GAME

Whether as a draft prospect or a "walk-on," players need to make the leap from the list to the game. As Donovan's story proves it can still be a big leap. CHL training camps are serious business. One young player admitted that the camp was the hardest, most intense experience of his fledgling hockey career.

A Coach's Perspective: *Parry Shockey, Regina Pats*

It may still be a gorgeous summer day but players are hitting the ice when August rolls around. Not for a warmup but to try out for a new season. Regina Pat's coach Parry Shockey provides some insight into what goes on at a training camp. For hotshot players he cautions that there are no givens, it really is an assessment.

There is a core of players you expect to make it but players have to make the team every year. Players bring in a talent base and you have to see where they fit in the team's game plan. Sometimes you see a player you do not expect to make it come into a camp and just hang on. You keep thinking you will cut him but every day he impresses you enough to keep him in the game.

There is a protected list of fifty players for each team and every year four or five players are deleted and new players added. Some players are late bloomers and some players who appear to have lots of potential never really step up. Older players are not immune to getting cut; sometimes you have to make room for new talent. Of the fifty players only half will be playing that season.

If this coach has a word of caution it is that first impressions are lasting impressions and you have to go into camp ready to give your best performance.

GOING TO CAMP: PLAYERS' PERSPECTIVES

Making the Team: An Eighth-Rounder With Attitude

An eight-round pick in the QMJHL Draft, Alex Johnstone wanted to earn a spot with the Mooseheads. When you are taken in the later rounds you are considered an outside chance. Alex spent the summer preparing to make a big impression. He worked hard on his conditioning and skills development so he would be ready. Major Junior would be a big step up but it was one he wanted to make.

All the other drafted players at camp had been selected in earlier rounds but Alex was determined to prove that he could contribute. His preparation paid off with a spot on the bench. He credits winning the spot to work ethic and heart.

During the early part of the season Alex spent a lot of time on that bench. He kept working and in his second season with the team logged regular ice time and was temporarily named captain when the team's captain was injured.

Making a Good Impression: a First-Rounder

Bryan Allen was a first-round pick of the Oshawa Generals in the OHL Entry Draft and he was expected to make the team. That did not stop him from training hard during the summer. He is well aware that there are no guarantees. The sixteen-year-old had actually been able to attend a training camp the previous summer. When a few players were no-shows at the Kingston Frontenacs' camp Bryan was invited to attend.

Growing up in a community near Kingston, Bryan was familiar with the team but it was not the same as sharing ice with OHL players. It is pretty impressive to see top NHL draft picks and to get the opportunity to play with them. When Bryan attended the Frontenacs camp, centre Chad Kilger had just been drafted fourth overall in the 1995 NHL Entry Draft. It is exciting and a bit intimidating to play with that calibre of player. The four days he spent with the Frontenacs meant that Bryan was able to go to the Generals camp with a bit of experience.

Oshawa prospects are divided into two teams when they arrive at camp; red and white. The teams alternate ice time. After being assigned a team the players head for the gym and fitness testing. Everything about the camp is intense, players are fighting to earn a spot and that means everyone is working hard.

Players are on the ice twice a day. In between the players will do workouts with the trainer. The trainer makes sure that players are stretching properly and not building up lactic acid in their muscles. The intense physical demands make summer training critical. Bryan worked very hard to come into camp in shape.

Bryan credits older players with helping the rookies make the adjustment. You usually don't talk to the coach much during the camp. Veteran players are a great source of information and motivation. It is an amazing feeling to play with top NHL prospects and realize that you can do it. The game is fast and intense but Bryan realized that he could play at this level.

After the third day of camp half the hopefuls are cut and the remainder get ready for the exhibition games. Once you start playing games you focus more on earning ice time in your position. The team tends to be light on veterans in the exhibition season because older players are away at pro camps. This gives rookies a chance to show their stuff.

Although the focus is hockey, players also need to deal with the new life off the ice. They are often in new cities and living with new families. As a first-rounder Bryan was assigned to billet with a family that expected to have him for the duration of the season. They were very welcoming and tried to make Bryan comfortable but there is some initial awkwardness when you live in a new home with strangers. Bryan was billeted with a roommate and he feels that doubling up is a great way to go. You have someone to talk to and hang out with who is in the same position.

There are some little things that are kind of fun. After years of buying sticks Bryan now just has to help himself to a stick from the team's supplies. You also get lots of other things like T-shirts and track suits. The team will also provide gear if there is something that a player needs. Bryan wore his own gear to camp. It is an intense couple of days and it helps to be completely comfortable.

Doing the Math: Sixty Prospects and Twenty-four Positions

Mathieu Biron was a Shawinigan Cataractes draft prospect. He was a third-round selection in the QMJHL Midget Draft. The first year he went to camp there were a lot of veterans on the ice. Of the ten defencemen looking for a spot on the roster seven were veterans. Mathieu went home. He was not overly upset with failing to crack the lineup. The rookie who made the team spent a lot of time on the bench and Mathieu got lots of ice time with his Midget team.

The second year was a different story; Mathieu wanted a spot on the roster. There were sixty players, each hoping to get his name on a jersey. Fortunately, this year was a big year for rookies, and the team had room for ten rookies in its lineup. That meant big chances at training camp.

Camp was a very intense experience. Mathieu indicates that those three days are some of the toughest you will ever face. A player has a lot to prove and three short days to do it. The team has on-ice training, off-ice training and scrimmages. Players play two games per day. Mathieu knew some of the veterans from his trip to camp the previous season but camp is not a very social place. He worked hard and then he slept.

The experience was exhausting. Players absolutely had to show up in shape. Mathieu trained regularly all summer. He logged lots of time in the gym and each week his agent would arrange for ice time so he could keep up his skills.

After three days the first cuts were made and about half the players headed home. The remaining thirty players were trimmed after some exhibition games. Mathieu was one of the players who earned a spot on the team but getting on the team is still only a step. With six rookie defencemen and only one veteran, a rookie can see lots of ice time, but you have to play well to earn it.

MOVING TO THE NEXT LEVEL

Making the cut gets the player on the roster. Staying there and getting more than a good view of the ice is going to take even more work. The CHL is recognized as a developmental league because it helps players move their game to the next level. Players need to come into the league willing to learn and work on improving their game. Teams provide assistance to players in the form of team trainers and special skills training. The next chapter provides a glimpse at the discipline and hard work it takes to be in game shape and the importance of improving your skill level.

Chapter 9
TRAINING AND CONDITIONING

BEING AN ELITE PLAYER is a big commitment. The higher the level of play the greater the demands on the athlete. It means having the discipline to hit the gym, foregoing certain foods, and having the humility and the patience to improve your skill level. If you want to be a prospect you have to be willing to make that commitment. This chapter looks at the effort junior players make to improve their conditioning and their skills.

BEING A BETTER ATHLETE: CONDITIONING

Players who want to play the best possible game are watching their diets and committing to conditioning. That means education and discipline. Major Junior players get some help in this department from the trainers employed by their teams.

Steve "Stu" Oviatt
Trainer, Kelowna Rockets
Photograph courtesy of the Kelowna Rockets

Player Support: Being a Trainer

Steve "Stu" Oviatt is the head trainer of the Kelowna Rockets of the WHL. In this league a head trainer fills a lot of shoes. He does everything from dealing with equipment, to handling medical problems, to providing nutritional guidelines. Players who are injured can count on Stu for quick treatment and assistance rehabbing until they are ready to get back in the game.

At this level he is an important resource to players. Learning proper technique and nutritional habits is critical to players becoming effective athletes. Stu develops the summer training program that all the players on the team's fifty-player protected list receive.

As an American growing up in Ohio, Stu came late to Canada's favourite pastime. He grew up an avid soccer player. When he originally started classes at Western Washington University he planned a career in the health professions, medicine or physiotherapy. Stu developed an interest in athletic training and loaded up on courses in sports psychology, nutrition and training.

Stu entered the WHL as a trainer with the Tacoma Rockets. He had worked with the Bellingham Ice Hawks and when the Rockets needed a trainer they approached Stu. The team was in Tacoma for two years before moving north to Kelowna. Stu saw the job as an opportunity to work with a group of elite athletes. He has been with the team for five years.

Being a full-time trainer doesn't mean he has stopped sharpening his skills. During one summer he received certification from the National Athletic Certification program and planned to become certified as a strength coach in the summer of 1998. It is important to ensure that

Steve "Stu" Oviatt – Stu helps goaltender Chris Noble
Photograph courtesy of the Kelowna Rockets Hockey Club

players are receiving the best treatment and advice and that means keeping up in the field, a field that is exploding as sports becomes a science and players are under continuous pressure to improve.

Fitness Testing

The first thing Stu does with new players who are coming into camp is fitness testing. The tests are oriented to the same criteria that the NHL uses to test its prospects. Testing includes testing the power, anaerobic capacity, aerobic capacity, weight, and percentage body fat of players. The results of these tests can help a player address weaknesses before the NHL tests come up.

Tests are performed three times in a season: when players come to camp, mid-season and post-season. This gives players a way to measure their conditioning throughout the year. The biggest surprise for young players is usually body fat. Appearances can be deceptive. A 210-pound player can have a low percentage of body fat and a 175-pound player can have a high percentage of body fat. The testing opens players' eyes to weaknesses in their training and conditioning.

Stu also gives the players some parameters. The NHL does fitness testing at the Entry Draft and Stu gives players the average values for the various tests. This allows players to compare themselves to NHL prospects. A player with dreams of being a professional athlete must make a commitment to a healthy lifestyle.

Player's Perspective: *Jeff Zehr, Erie Otters*

Learning proper training technique may be time-consuming, but it is worth the effort. Jeff Zehr became a conditioning convert early in his career. A high school gym teacher who was also a personal trainer clued Jeff in to the importance of training properly. Jeff admits that at first he felt a little foolish and it was awkward to work out with a trainer. It took some time before he really bought into the importance of training.

When Jeff made the transition to Junior he realized he needed to get stronger if he wanted to be successful. That realization was part of his motivation to improve his strength and conditioning. He wanted to maximize his workouts and that meant educating himself.

During his rookie season with the Spitfires he was too tired to do much in the way of off-ice conditioning. Like so many first year players the time between school, practice and games was for sleeping. During the summers Jeff used to follow a personal program designed by Leafs trainer Chris Broadhurst. Now that he has been drafted by the New York Islanders they design his programs.

Jeff Zehr – Erie Otters
Photograph courtesy of Jim Cooper and the Erie Otters

After his rookie season Jeff increased his in-season training. In a typical week he hits the gym at least twice a week. He admits it can be hard to make the time but sees it as something you have to do. He and some equally-dedicated teammates often train together. Jeff usually rides the exercise bike to get his cardio workout. He switches his workouts around, sometimes doing long-duration aerobic activities like biking or running and other days doing sprint intervals.

Jeff also lifts weights. He does a lot of work on upper body, chest, arms and shoulders. He keeps the weight light. He is not interested in "bulking up." He knows that will come with age; right now he is focused on getting stronger. Jeff starts every workout with a warmup, which includes stretching, for about ten minutes.

Final comments on training from this prospect: "I think the training, the discipline, trying and wanting to improve myself, getting up early . . . it helped me dedicate myself to the game."

During the Season

When it comes to off-ice training the work that players do during the year is more maintenance than conditioning. Players have school, practices and games, leaving little time for serious conditioning. During the occasional week without a game, trainer Stu Oviatt will work in some foot-speed drills and maintenance endurance exercises. Stu will also help individual players set up weight training routines. His biggest responsibility during the season is working with injured players. He focuses on specific exercises to rehabilitate and strengthen the player after an injury.

Periodization

Strength and conditioning are critical to being a successful athlete. When it comes to this type of training a key concept is periodization. The year is broken up for players into in-season, off-season, and pre-season training. The appropriate type of training depends on which phase a player is in.

When the season ends Stu recommends taking a couple of weeks to relax. Your body needs recovery time. Take three or four weeks to let your batteries recharge before starting an off-season program. During the off-season players can focus on rebuilding and heavy strengthening. Stu recommends against heavy weight lifting for very young players.

Hockey is a demanding sport that requires explosive speed, endurance, strength, flexibility, and cardio conditioning. When he puts together a program for players Stu focuses on incorporating these different elements. Players at the Major Junior level need a weight program and a conditioning program.

Player's Perspective: *Jay Henderson, Edmonton Ice*

The Ice's Jay Henderson stays in shape during the season by riding the exercise bike and lifting weights when he can squeeze in the time. Between school, practices and games it is a tight squeeze. Like so many players, most of Jay's training is done in the off season.

In the summer this 5'11", 170-pound left wing hits the Panther Gym in downtown Edmonton five times a week. He does a balanced workout that includes cardio, boxing, weightlifting, and stretching. Boxing involves anaerobic conditioning, interval training and foot speed which makes it a great workout for a hockey player.

Jay isn't left to his own devices when it comes to training. There is a special program for the players designed and approved by the team. Jay's dedication to conditioning is a testament to his commitment to the sport. There is not much "off" to his off-season but he knows that there will be physical testing when he returns to camp.

Starting to sound like a lot of work? Jay knows that hockey involves sacrifice but when you love something you dig in and work for it and Jay loves the game. Does the hard work pay off? With twenty points in the first sixteen games of the 1997-98 season it looks like Jay came off the summer in great shape. Jay managed to lead his team in points all season and earn a contract with his NHL club, the Boston Bruins.

The Summer Program

Away from the watchful eye of their teams, players need discipline and commitment to train during the summer. Stu is always available to players who call with questions or training concerns. He also provides a comprehensive summer program for the players.

The program is both general and specific. When they return home players have different resources available and Stu needs to make a program that anyone can use. He provides a number of alternatives within specific types of training. For example, when it comes to cardio conditioning some players prefer to ride a bike, others prefer to run. Some players have access to gyms in their home towns and others have some free weights in the basement. Stu creates a program that is adaptable to the resources available to players.

The program designed by Stu Oviatt for the Kelowna Rockets contains three basic types of exercises—weight lifting, aerobic and plyometrics. The program also provides information on the stretching a player should be doing and a reminder that players should stretch prior to all daily workouts. The program requires players to exercise five days per week.

When it comes to weight lifting, the program advises a balanced schedule and encourages working different body parts on different days. The one exception is abdominal exercises, which are included in all sessions. Stu provides information on weight-lifting exercises for the chest, biceps, wrists, shoulders, triceps, lats, quadriceps, hamstrings and calves.

The summer is broken down into three phases. In the early part of the summer players do a low-intensity, high-repetitions weight program. During the second part of the summer players do medium intensity, medium repetitions. At the end of the summer, players switch to a high-intensity, low-repetitions workout.

Stu allows players a great deal of flexibility in choosing their random aerobic activities. Sports like golf, baseball and soccer and activities like swimming, step machines, rowing and biking all qualify to satisfy the aerobic portion of the player's exercise program. Players can pick any activity they enjoy as long as they continue for forty-five minutes.

In addition to the random aerobic activity that players are expected to do twice per week, players have specific running/walking requirements on the three weight-lifting days. Stu designs these requirements to help players achieve different goals. In the early portion of the summer the focus is on increasing endurance capacity, the second part of the summer focuses on increasing speed and in the final part of the summer the program's focus switches to increasing explosiveness.

It is during the final portion of the summer that plyometrics become incorporated into the program. Plyometrics are exercises that help a player develop quickness and agility. They involve jumping and rapid foot movements. An example of a plyometric exercise in Stu's summer program is vertical leaps. Players squat about ninety degrees and leap as high as possible. Players must land lightly and repeat the leap.

This program provides an overview of the type of training that Major Junior players undertake to ensure that they come to camp in shape and ready for the season. This is a program designed for seventeen-to-twenty-year-old Major Junior players and is undertaken with the consultation of their trainer.

Stu reminds any young players interested in training for hockey that it is important to speak to a physician before you begin a training program. When you have been cleared to begin, remember that proper technique is critical to training successfully and without injury.

For young players interested in learning to train effectively there are professionals who can be consulted. Doctors, physiotherapists, athletic therapists, and personal trainers may be able to provide guidance or programs for young athletes. There are also books and other information available on nutrition and proper conditioning. Your family doctor can be a great source of information.

Player's Perspective: *Alex Johnstone, Halifax Mooseheads*

Alex Johnstone trained diligently the summer before he made the Halifax Mooseheads. After a seventy-eight-game regular season and eighteen playoff games he needed a rest. The first few weeks of the summer were down time. Alex relaxed and caught up on his sleep. Refreshed, he got back into the off-season conditioning phase.

During the summer, Alex uses a personal trainer. His trainer was a boxer and he had a copy of the New York Rangers' summer training program. Alex worked out four to five times per week. He admits it wasn't always easy finding the discipline to go to the gym. Alex likes to get into a routine. If he doesn't have a regular schedule it gets easy for him to miss workouts.

The goal for the summer was to gain some muscle. With the help of his trainer, Alex was able to add twelve pounds to his six-foot frame. Alex didn't just want to bulk up, he wanted to improve his game. The main focus of his workout was legs. Strong legs are a big part of being a strong skater. Alex trained his legs twice per week. On other days he would work biceps, chest, back and triceps. He sees older players and knows there is a natural "filling out" process.

During the off-season he did higher weights and lower repetitions to build muscle. Alex's trainer helped ensure that he used proper technique. The regular season is tough and during Alex's first year with the team he was too tired to do much individual training. This is a common occurrence for young rookies.

In his second and draft-eligible year Alex kept up his workouts. There are physical tests to face at the end of the season and he wanted to be in good shape. He switched some components of his workout for the in-season phase. Instead of weight training he does circuit training for endurance. He has cut back on leg workouts because skating is a great workout and he gets lots of ice time.

Conditioning is an important part of the game for Alex. Conditioning makes him a better athlete. This league is demanding; players play very hard. To keep up you need to keep in shape.

Topping Up the Tanks: Fueling Athletes

The body is a big tool and it needs proper fuel to run efficiently. Players are quick to realize how connected eating habits are to performance. Stu offers some guidance when it comes to pre-game meals. What you eat just before a game is not your fuel. It is what sits in your stomach and digests. The harder your pre-game meal is to digest the more blood is diverted from your hard-working muscles. Does that mean you should play on an empty stomach? No. If you do you will feel sluggish and will perform poorly.

The pre-game meal should be light and easy to digest. Stu recommends eating several hours before the game and topping up the tank with things like granola bars or fruit until game time. You should not feel full when you hit the ice but a growling stomach can be a big distraction.

The meal that ends up as fuel for the game is actually the one eaten several hours before the game. This

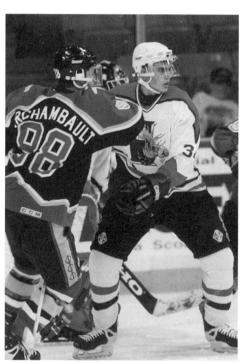

Alex Johnstone – Halifax Mooseheads
Photograph courtesy of Terry Waterfield

food will have been digested and made available for energy. The best source of energy is complex carbohydrates. Many junior players cite foods like spaghetti and lasagna as their favourites. Pasta, potatoes, fruits and vegetables are excellent sources of energy for young players. Chocolate bars may seem like a good pick-me-up but quick-fix sugar rushes are short-lived and players are left feeling sluggish.

Nutritional concerns do not end when the final buzzer sounds. With a seventy-plus game schedule there is usually another game looming. Games are intense and deplete players' energy stores; rebuilding should begin immediately. For a brief period immediately after a game a player's muscles are open to refueling. A quick healthy snack like a piece of fruit, some juice or a granola bar will help the player recover.

Players' Perspectives On Food

Erie Otters Jeff Zehr made the connection between fuel and performance. With a low body fat ratio, Jeff is in top condition. He trains diligently but is also careful about what he eats. He prepares his own breakfast and lunch. He incorporates healthy snacking into his day. The effort required to plan and prepare meals and snacks may seem like a lot of work but to Jeff it is worth it. This Islanders' prospect is committed to being a career athlete and if it means logging some time in the kitchen, he's up for it.

These days he is getting some nutritional guidance. The Islanders have a nutritionist who checks on their prospects' eating habits and offers suggestions and recipes. Jeff is not a light eater. By his own admission he can eat "tonnes of food." It isn't the quantity that is a concern, it is the quality. He is a very healthy eater.

Alex Johnstone was quick to figure out that grease and games did not go well together. He avoids greasy foods noting that they tend to "sit in his stomach." He does admit to the occasional indulgence. An important part of indulging for him is knowing when he can afford it. Alex knows his game schedule and is careful about pre-game nutrition. If friends suggest grabbing a slice at pizza corner Alex will consider the impact on his game and will often forgo the snack and grab something healthier when he gets home.

Drink Up: The Importance Of Proper Hydration

Water is very important to young athletes. You will be dehydrated long before you begin to feel thirsty. One player noted that after a five-game stint he had lost ten pounds. This type of weight loss is actually water loss. Your body replaces fluids more slowly than they are lost through sweat. To keep from getting too far behind, drink up. Drink before, during and after games or workouts. Obviously you should not drink until you give yourself a sore stomach but do drink as much as you comfortably can.

DEVELOPING YOUR HOCKEY SKILLS

Being in good condition is important but players are also focusing on developing their skills. All across the country skills clinics and hockey schools have sprung up to answer the desire of players to improve. Unfortunately, judging the quality of a program can be very difficult for parents and players.

This segment has two parts. The first part looks at one of the most fundamental skills, skating. Edmonton Oilers' skating instructor Steffany Hanlen offers some tips to young players. The second part of the segment offers some guidance on getting the best value when a player enrolls in a skills program.

Steffany Hanlen – Skating Instructor
Photograph courtesy of Hanlen Consulting

Being a Better Skater

If you want to be a hockey player you have to know how to skate. The game gets faster the higher you advance and that means you need strong skating skills to keep up. Steffany Hanlen knows a lot about skating. Since 1979 she has been a skating instructor for hockey players. Although her company, Hanlen Consulting, has programs for all ages, Steffany focuses on her work with professional players.

Steffany regularly works with the Edmonton Oilers and the WHL's Edmonton Ice. During the summer she also works with other top players. At this level she mostly does one-on-one work with the athlete. She assesses the player's skating and works on improving both technique and skating-specific conditioning. In addition to her work with players she has also produced a manual, *A Progressive Guide To Efficient and Effective Skating for Hockey Players*.

Even top athletes can have bad habits that weaken their skating. Steffany has worked with players who were amazed at how much they improved. It is often the athletes themselves who come looking for assistance. Steffany worked with an Oiler who was a first-rounder in the draft and he was amazed by what he didn't know about how skating effectively can relate to hockey. Players who come to Steffany have often plateaued and are trying to get better. In some cases coaches notice problems and encourage players to get assistance.

Since being a competitive athlete is time-consuming, players come to Steffany eager to get their problems resolved and get back in the game. Steffany will do an assessment and can usually fix their problems in a couple of sessions. After that it becomes maintenance. It is the maintenance that requires the most effort and Steffany notes that athletes who want the improvement make the commitment.

Despite her success in the field, Steffany makes no claim to having a secret to success. She is quick to point out there is no secret method. Skating is a matter of physics, blades on ice, and bodies in motion and good communication between instructor and player.

Common Errors and Helpful Hints

Steffany sees a lot of players but the problems are similar. Problems can involve more than technique—improper equipment or lack of muscular strength can also affect performance. This segment provides some helpful tips for young skaters seeking to improve their performance.

Equipment Errors: Skates

When it comes to equipment one of the biggest mistakes Steffany sees is poorly-fitted skates. Skates should not fit like sneakers. Players should not be able to stick a finger behind the heel. Loose-fitting skates means there is movement in the boot that is not transferred to the blade. The only purpose the boot serves is to connect the foot to the blade. To accomplish that players need snug skates.

Players often stand up when they try on skates but that is not how you skate. When you try on a skate bend your knees the way you would if you were skating. Your heel should be in the back of the boot. A snug fit may take some getting used to but players make the change when they know it will improve their performance.

Another important thing to look at in selecting skates is the stiffness of the boot. Ankle bend is important to skating and a boot that is too stiff interferes with this important function. Stress that should be absorbed by the bending in your ankle shoots straight up your leg. This can increase overuse injuries.

The Tall and the Short Of It

Steffany does not teach a standard technique. A player's technique is related to size, strength and body type. She points out that Eric Lindros doesn't skate like Theo Fleury and she doesn't expect or train her players to skate the same. She helps them to skate the best way for them.

Looking for the perfect technique can be a problem for young players. They may end up trying to adopt a technique that is not suited to their body type. One problem Steffany has noticed is smaller players trying to skate like taller players. The player is taking over-long strides and that is less efficient. Steffany notes that overall, shorter players tend to be stronger skaters because they have had to be to keep up with the game.

Taller players do take longer strides and that means moving across the ice with less effort. That can also mean that as the players advance to faster levels of play they get left behind. It has been easier for them so they haven't had to maximize their performance. That may mean lack of muscular strength or it may mean improper technique. Sometimes taller skaters stand up more and take shorter strides.

Common Errors In Technique

While technique depends on personal factors there are some common elements. Steffany sees some errors over and over again. One frequent problem is a stance that is too wide. Another common problem is players who skate with their bodies upright. Proper technique means knees bent and that is why skating, when it is done properly, is such a good workout for your legs. It is also what makes it hard work.

It is simple—bend your knees, bend your knees more. It is a very basic but important concept. It means hard work and a lazy player often avoids it by bending over at the waist. This is bad form and bad for your back. In conditioning exercises, Steffany keeps inventing ways to disguise knee bend drills. Success means effort and fundamentals.

Another common problem is enthusiastic arm swinging. There is a proper way to use your upper body. Swinging your arms side to side like a gorilla is not it. Steffany notes that it goes right back to basic physics. Your body is being propelled forward; swinging your arms from side to side interferes with that forward motion. Arms should be moving in line with the body and in the direction the body is moving.

These problems seem simple enough so you are probably wondering why they haven't been corrected already. Players do not watch themselves play. They may have every confidence they are skating like Coffey when they look like King Kong on skates. To correct their technique players must be aware of how they move.

Modern technology makes that easy. Steffany often videotapes players to show them exactly how they look when they skate. She can point out the problems to players and show them proper techniques, but players have to make the change. This change involves commitment and self-assessment.

GETTING THE BEST VALUE: TIPS TO ASSESS SKATING PROGRAMS

Things to Look for In an Instructor

Hockey has always been a national pastime but as salaries escalate and more and more teams join the NHL, the level of investment made by young prospects has increased. Chasing the Dream can be an expensive proposition. Steffany notes that you can't turn around in Canada without seeing a new hockey school, skills program or trainer. As a nineteen-year veteran in the field Steffany has some practical advice to offer parents and players when it comes to choosing a skating program.

Skating for Hockey

There is no official certification for an instructor in power skating. Some instructors are former players, others, like Steffany, are former figure skaters. Steffany has a background in figure skating but she has some words of caution when it comes to using an instructor who is a figure skater. Hockey is hockey. That means pucks and sticks. Training a player to skate without factoring in these hockey essentials is not effective. Skating with a stick introduces a different dynamic.

The ultimate focus should always be skating as a part of the game. A good instructor has to acknowledge the game, not just the skating. Steffany breaks down the game into components and works to make her clients more effective players. In addition to checking whether the instructor will be using sticks and pucks it is also a good idea to check the instructor's skates. Hockey skates and figure skates are not the same.

Being a Teacher

Being an instructor means being a teacher. Former players may have been very good at the game but that is no guarantee that they can teach. Check for a background in physical education. Ask former clients and try to get information from players who are the same age and level of ability as yourself.

Getting What You Pay for

Checking an instructor may involve looking at more than one individual. Hockey schools may have several instructors and during a week-long program the players may work with different people. Parents and players have a right to know who will be instructing and for what amount of time.

A big-name instructor may spend only an hour on the ice in a week-long program. That might not be a bad thing; the regular instructors may be very competent. The issue is getting what you pay for. Steffany does group seminars. The type of instructing she does is very different than her one-on-one player consulting program. She is careful to ensure that players and parents understand what they are getting.

Getting What You Want

Getting what you want means knowing what you want. Parents may want a recreational program for their child. In other situations players may want to improve their skills level because they are hoping to play at an elite level. Price varies depending on what type of instruction a player is getting. Parents should research the programs and find one tailored to their child's needs. Steffany cautions that ice costs and instructor costs vary from centre to centre; you cannot compare apples to oranges.

Doing the Research

Steffany does not depend on advertising for her business. Word of mouth and reputation bring in her clientele. If you want to know about a program or an instructor ask around. If you can, attend a few classes and talk to parents and players. An instructor should be receptive to questions from a prospective client. Ask for specific information on the services being offered and the instructor's credentials. Taking the time to properly research options means a greater chance of being satisfied with your choice.

Getting the Most Out Of It

Canada is a predominantly rural country. Hockey schools often pass through communities or players travel considerable distances to attend the programs. Steffany offers some tips for getting the most out of your sessions.

Steffany will help players learn technique but unless the technique is practiced consistently it is of little benefit. To get the most out of investing in a skating program, go in ready to learn. Steffany encourages parents and players to take notes and/or videotape sessions. She has no problem with parents attending sessions. This is particularly helpful with younger players who may not remember all the details later.

Chapter 10
BEHIND THE BENCH: COACHES ON COACHING

COACHING A CHL TEAM is serious business. Like NHL coaches, CHL coaches need strong performances and there is no guarantee of job security. Young prospects will be faced with professional coaches who are making tough decisions.

This chapter will help players get a glimpse behind the bench. What does the job entail? What you can do to impress your coach?

Three coaches express their opinions on the game, the job and the players. Former Vancouver Canucks coach Tom Renney shares his experiences as a coach in the WHL and the NHL. Real Paiement has coached three QMJHL teams, Chicoutimi, Granby and Moncton. He was also the head coach of the 1997 National Junior Team. Parry Shockey coached the Lethbridge Hurricanes to a league championship in 1996-97 and in the 1997-98 season he took over as head coach for the Regina Pats.

A coach has to be ready for hard work and book work. The willingness to relocate is a must for this profession. All three coaches have been certified and regularly attend symposiums to keep up with new developments in the sport. They all have something else in common; they love the game and they love what they do.

GETTING BEHIND THE BENCH
Tom Renney: From Junior "B" To the NHL

There aren't many people who would turn down the chance to coach an NHL team. The real question is: how do you get the offer? Being a coach is an occupational choice and it requires the same commitment and training as any other job. This native of Cranbrook, B.C. started out like so many young Canadians—on the ice. Renney played Junior "B" and college hockey. He has a tremendous love of the game and his life is a testament to that.

He realized early on that a smallish skilled defenceman wasn't what the NHL was looking for. So what's a hockey lover to do? For Renney the love of the game found expression in coaching. Renney had good coaches during his playing years and attributes their influence to his interest in coaching.

Is hockey all he knows? No, he has a degree in physical education from the University of North Dakota. To better prepare himself as a coach Renney availed himself of the training provided by the National Coaching Certification Program. He went through all five levels offered by the program. His opportunities were enhanced by the training and certification.

Anyone coaching a rep team has to have at least intermediate training, the equivalent of what was then Level Three. Since Renney went on to coach Canada's most representative team—our national team—it looks like time well spent. Renney endorsed the NCC program as an opportunity to get guidance and practical coaching advice. He concedes that a day or two at a program won't make a coach but he believes it will make a better coach.

Renney's climb to the NHL began in 1983 when he became the coach of the Junior "B" team in Trail B.C. He later coached in Invermere, B.C. Having had a taste of it, Renney decided to focus on coaching and accepted a position with the Penticton Knights. At one point he almost ended his coaching career by taking an administrative position that kept him in hockey, but behind a desk. With a young family to raise, Renney decided to give the job a shot. After a year he decided that coaching was what he really wanted to be doing.

An opportunity came up when Ken Hitchcock, now the coach of the Dallas Stars, left his job as head coach in Kamloops. Renney jumped at the chance to coach the Blazers. This would be a big step and a trial to see if he would pursue coaching as a career. Packing up his family Renney headed for Kamloops.

In his first year with the Kamloops Blazers Renney was awarded the WHL Coach of the Year award. He modestly attributes the award to the quality of the team, which had a record season and a pennant win. The awards committee definitely knew what they were doing, because next year Renney led his team to a Memorial Cup victory.

After Kamloops Renney became a coach for the national team. He had to make room for an Olympic silver medal (1993-94), and World Championship bronze (1994-95) and silver (1995-96) in his trophy case.

The management of the Vancouver Canucks obviously felt that Renney was a coach with potential, because on June 4, 1996 he was named head coach.

Real Paiement: Have Passport, Will Coach

To follow Paiement's career in hockey you need a map and a passport. He has seen a lot of games in a lot of leagues in a lot of countries. Paiement got his first taste of coaching early. He was the captain of the Junior Canadiens and when the coach couldn't make a practice he would lead his teammates through the drills. Paiement's playing career continued in Milwaukee with the International Hockey League (IHL). After Milwaukee he played in France for a year before coming back to McGill University. He got another taste of coaching in Europe since most players had to coach as well as play.

Although he started at McGill as a player it was also to be his first official coaching job. He was an assistant coach with the team for two years. He also worked on a degree in Industrial Relations. Despite working for a year with IBM, he made coaching his career choice. After McGill, Paiement coached Tier II in Montreal before taking on his first QMJHL team, the Granby Predateurs. He remained there as head coach for three-and-a-half years.

After his stint in Granby, he once again headed to Europe, this time to coach an "A" league team in Brunico, Italy. Although he had an assistant coach who could translate, Paiement quickly learned how to communicate. Speaking with players is important; if you have to wait around for the translation you lose the impact.

After Italy, Paiement headed back to Canada, this time to the University of Trois-Rivières, Quebec, where he remained for two seasons before heading to Chicoutimi. During his second and final season he led that team to the Memorial Cup Championship.

The frequent flyer miles on this coach have taken him to his new and current home in Moncton, New Brunswick where he is now head coach of the Moncton Wildcats. Does this mean his traveling days are over? Well, as head coach of the National Junior team he won't be putting away that passport quite yet.

So does the coach like coaching or just traveling? He doesn't just like it, he loves it. He loved playing and when he realized he wasn't good enough to keep going as a player he became a coach. Paiement insists, "I love the game. To do anything properly you have to have a passion for it."

Paiement takes coaching very seriously. He has currently completed Level Three of the National Coaching Certification. He is ready to get

Level Four and plans to present to the committee of experts in Spokane. Level Four requires twelve tasks, completed over a period of two years. You have to present your physical, mental and technical preparations. In addition to pursuing his certification levels Paiement regularly attends coaching seminars and keeps up with new material in the field.

Parry Shockey: Player, Parent, Coach

Shockey was another coach who started out playing and quickly realized that he would not be making one of the then six NHL teams in the league. His first coaching experience was with junior hockey but he found he was too close in age to the players and decided to get back in the game. He played senior hockey in Alberta for five years. In his last year the coach/general manager was killed in a car accident and Shockey took over the coaching and managing function of the team.

In 1975-76 Shockey took on coaching a midget team. It was a tough group but Shockey was up to the challenge and took the team to the Provincials. Shockey had always been interested in coaching younger players. He went from his midget team to coaching an AAA Peewee team in Lethbridge, Alberta. Despite the young age of the players it was a tough gig. It was a traveling team with a number of practices. Shockey stayed with this team for three years before moving on to coach an AAA Midget team in Lethbridge. He was with this team for three years.

Shockey applied for a position as an assistant coach with the Lethbridge Hurricanes and didn't get the job. This setback precipitated a re-assessment. Like so many coaches Shockey considered getting out. But like so many coaches with passion and talent he decided to stay in the game. He headed to the University of Lethbridge where he was the assistant coach to Mike Babcock. The team went to Nationals that year and won the CIAU championships.

An opportunity opened up in Major Junior for Shockey in Spokane so he packed up and headed to Washington. He finished the remainder of the season with the team. That summer Mike Babcock was hired as the coach and Shockey stayed for another two years as assistant coach.

In 1996-97 another opportunity opened up in the league and Shockey headed back to Lethbridge. After two-and-a-half years of living apart from his family he was finally heading home. That year saw the Hurricanes win the WHL championships and go to the Memorial Cup tournament. After his success with the Hurricanes Shockey decided to take on a new challenge and headed to Regina to coach the Pats.

Like so many good coaches he does more than just move from team to team. Shockey has his advanced level certification and regularly attends symposiums. He recognizes that the game is expanding and that he has to stay on the leading edge, an edge he observes has become a fine line. It's all part of keeping up in his chosen field. No technophobe, this coach uses a computer both to provide information and as a tool to assist in preparation for the season.

GETTING THE JOB DONE: RENNEY GETS DOWN TO BUSINESS

How does this coach see himself? Renney describes himself as basically a teacher, and credits his communication skills with much of his success. He can make players understand what he wants. He recognizes that criticism is an important part of his role but is emphatic that constructive criticism should be developmental and not cruel. Sarcasm can cut very deeply and coaches need to be aware of that particularly with young players. Belittling or degrading players is inappropriate.

Well, It's Not the NHL, But . . . .

The CHL is a proving ground for players and for coaches. Having coached at both levels Renney recognizes that there are differences between the NHL and its younger sibling. On a plus side for coaching he notes that the younger players are more pliable, more willing to take instruction.

When he was in the WHL he tried to sit down with junior players and explain his game philosophy. Major Junior is a developmental league and a coach has a responsibility to do everything he can to help his players develop. This means more than hockey, it means developing well-rounded young men who have as many options as possible available to them.

A coach in the WHL doesn't have the same size staff as the NHL; Renney is more directly involved in helping players develop, including arranging conditioning programs, and skills training to improve everything from agility to foot speed to mental skills—whatever it takes to help players reach their potential. The Major Junior teams aren't without support. They just go to outside sources if the developmental needs cannot be met by the team's staff.

You Got to Know When to Play Them

Being a good coach also means knowing when a young player is ready to take his place on the ice. Renney recognizes that it is easy to get caught up in an exciting new prospect. You can't kid yourself that a player is ready when he is not. Trying to push the player too early can be detrimental to his development. Deciding the proper time to play a player is the coach's call. Renney says one of the reasons Kamloops is so successful is their careful absorption of new players, usually at the rate of four rookies a year.

Establishing Rapport With Your Team

Once you have your team you need to convince them to play your way. A coach needs to build a relationship with his team. According to Renney if you want the players to buy into your coaching philosophy you need to have a rapport with the team. A team always has leaders, players who are respected and looked to as role models. To be an effective coach you need to build a relationship with these players. If these players believe in the coach they can help deliver the message to their teammates and generate commitment within the team.

And Their Parents

There are more than players involved in Major Junior hockey; there are also the parents. Part of the coach's responsibility is to sit down and speak with parents about the program and the player's abilities. It can be tough because parents are sometimes reluctant to accept anything less than a promise that junior will play first line. Those promises can rarely be made except maybe for a little Mario or Gretzky. Major Junior is a big step up for players. It is important to be honest about the reality of the league. All you can really promise is to work with the player to help him develop to the best of his abilities. It is critical not to build false expectations in parents or players.

What Does a Coach Do If a Player Isn't Going to Make It?

Sometimes Major Junior players just aren't going to make the big golden step to the NHL. Renney dealt with that early in his playing career, but how does he help his players deal with it? Renney's mandate is sincerity: treat the player the way you would want to be treated. If you were not going to make it how would you want to hear it? Renney is adamant that you have to be honest with the player. If the player has a fourth-line role let him know the implications of that role.

Does it mean there is never hope? No. Honest evaluation can sometimes steer a player to a better position or to becoming a role player. Maybe the player won't be the next Mario but could become a strong stay-at-home defenceman. Sometimes, no matter how hard the player works, it just isn't going to happen for him.

Coaches in the CHL occupy a starring role in young players' lives. They are role models, guidance counselors and surrogate fathers. Renney appreciates the responsibilities to players that comes with assuming a coaching position. When a player isn't going to make the NHL Renney sees his role as providing guidance about educational and other opportunities.

What other opportunities are there? Renney started out as a player and ended up as a coach. There is a bigger game in Major Junior—it's called getting players ready for LIFE. It's important for a coach to help players learn about their options. There are opportunities in hockey such as scouting and administration. Coaches can be an excellent resource for players.

Playing Favourites

Something maybe every player suspects is that coaches have favourites. Coaches are human; they do develop close relationships with players. As an example Renney cites Corey Hirsch. Renney has a long history with this player; they won the Memorial Cup together and Hirsch played on the national team. Unfortunately, Hirsch was ill last year and Renney had to wait to see how he did at camp. A team can have only so many goaltenders and a coach has to do what is best for the team. Coaching is a profession and if you make personal instead of professional choices you may end up looking for a new job.

Up With The Sun: a Day In the Life Of an NHL Coach

To interview Renney you have to get up early in the morning. He usually arrives at the arena about 6:30 a.m. and sits down to review the most recent game tape. After reviewing the tape Renney meets with his assistant coaches and brainstorms things that need to be done and players he will need to speak with. With the use of the tape he makes notes and when the players show up around 10:00 a.m. he will have a practice ready.

The players trickle in between 9:00 a.m. and 10:30 a.m., hitting the exercise room to lift weights, stretch or do some cardio. Renney takes the opportunity to speak to some players. Then it is time for the on-ice practice. This lasts about an hour. The players hit the showers and the coach hits the mikes. Renney explains that he spends fifteen to twenty minutes after practice answering questions from the media.

If it is not a game day the players head home but the coach has a lot more to do. The results of the practice have to be discussed and there is always the next game to prepare for. This involves an afternoon spent viewing tapes of opponents, discussing strategy with his staff and making game plans.

If it is not a game day Renney heads home at around 6:30 p.m. to spend some quiet time with his wife and two children. If it is a game day Renney takes up his position behind the bench. You might think that with all the preparation Renney can stand back and enjoy the game. Think again: hockey is unpredictable and from the first drop of the puck to the last buzzer it requires constant evaluation.

Renney has his game plan but he knows the game can change within minutes of the puck being dropped. That is what makes it exciting. Injuries or unpredictable behaviour can force rapid re-evaluation by a coach. That doesn't mean all the preparation is worthless: a good coach needs to know his players, his team and his opponents so he can make those quick decisions.

Does it sound like a long day? It is an even longer season. With the exhibition games starting early in the fall and the Stanley Cup playoffs going late into the spring it can be a long year for a coach. But summer does not mean it is time to kick back and relax. Renney has a team to build for next season.

LEAGUE CHAMPIONS 1996-97: PARRY SHOCKEY ON COACHING

Parry Shockey coached his team, the Lethbridge Hurricanes, to the Memorial Cup Tournament in 1997 but unfortunately they didn't come home with the cup. So what does it take to coach a team through the playoffs?

The Playoffs

Shockey has no magic formula to get a team to and through the playoffs. It's something he has been working on through the seventy-two games of the regular season. According to this coach, "You practice to play the real games. You play to play again." And play again his team did all the way to a league championship. By the time a team hits the playoffs it needs to be a well-oiled machine, fine-tuned through the regular season. If problems come up through the regular season the coach has to address them and cure them.

The league is divided into three divisions and the majority of games are played within the division. Shockey doesn't consider this a problem in preparing for the playoffs. Each team gets together at least twice with every other team so the team is used to different systems. Shockey thinks that hockey is a simple game and the important thing in coaching is to build a strong foundation on that simplicity.

The Memorial Cup

Despite a league championship, this team lost out on the Memorial Cup win. Shockey says that his disappointment is easier to deal with because he plans another assault on the cup. His disappointment was more for the players. Many of the players have aged out of the league and won't get another chance at winning this coveted trophy. Shockey says winning this cup is extremely difficult because of the rapid turnover of players in the league. A team has a narrow window of opportunity to build a strong team before the league age limits force them to start over again.

Trading for talent in Major Junior is as important as it is in the NHL. Shockey admits that getting Chris Phillips was a huge step in the team's drive to win. He also says that this kind of trading is something of a tradition in the league. Unlike the NHL where players can have a longer career, Major Junior players age out quickly. Phillips played well in Prince Albert but when the team wasn't going to make it to the playoffs they traded him for some young prospects. This gave Phillips the chance to go for the league championship and the Memorial Cup.

Adjusting To a New Team

After his success with Lethbridge, Shockey headed to Regina to coach the Regina Pats. What does a coach do to adjust to a new team? Shockey credits communication with the players as key to being successful with a new team. "You need to try to inform them as much as possible, where we want to go, set expectations, making sure the players know the goals." To do this you have to pay attention to the details. Players need to have good habits. Shockey recognizes that there is always an adjustment period when you start with a new team. Part of being an effective coach is knowing when you can bend and when to stand your ground.

THE WORLD JUNIOR CUP: REAL PAIEMENT ON COACHING

Getting the Job

Every young player wants to be at the World Junior Cup. They get scouted. If they are lucky they get invited to camp and if they are what the team needs they get the coveted Team Canada jersey. But what about the coach, how does he get selected? Well like so many jobs this one starts with an application. Of the applications tendered, ten are selected for interviews.

The interviews are no mere formality. As Paiement found out, they drilled him with questions. He admits his first year he wasn't quite prepared for the rigorous questioning. The second year he had prepared but of course they already knew the answers to the old questions so he faced a new round of questions. He was the assistant coach of the 1996 team. Third time is the charm and Paiement got the call to be the head coach of the 1997 team.

What is it about this coach that made him the choice to take on Canada's National Junior team? Preparation is a big part of this coach's game plan. You have to be organized and plan—plan the skills training, physical training—on ice and off ice. You prepare team-building activities, and create goals that get players together. Admittedly you have to be flexible enough to adapt your plans when necessary. Prioritization and time management are important because the league is so busy.

Another key component to being a good coach is knowledge. You have to know how to challenge players and develop them without draining them. Players are sophisticated; they know a lot and to maintain their respect, the coach has to know what he is doing.

The biggest compliment this coach ever received was from a player he cut as a nineteen-year-old. This player went on to play for Concordia University and told another coach that Paiement was the most honest coach he had ever met. Paiement is committed to honesty; he feels you need to let players know what their ice time will be. He admits that sometimes you lose a player because of that but it is better than having a frustrated player on the team.

This coach also stresses communication. You have to reach your players, tell them clearly what you expect, something Paiement can do in three languages. You always have to be careful because it's not what you say that's important, it is what they hear.

Getting Prepared

The coaching staff is named in June, which does not allow much time to prepare for the December tournament. Barry Trapp, the scout for this tournament, has already been scouring the league to select the fortunate forty players who will be invited to the August camp. Throughout the season players are evaluated and discussed by the coaching staff. You would think it would be easy to get the twenty-two best players in the league. Paiement debunks that myth: "The success of the team isn't getting the best twenty-two players; it is getting the twenty-two players you need to get the best team. They have to be willing to play in their roles."

You have gathered top players from all over the country and you need to get them functioning as a team in a short period of time. This requires team building. Sometimes the activities you plan are not the ones that really solidify the team. As a coach you always have to be open to opportunities for team building.

In 1996-97 team building took a funny twist for the national team. Their initial results were not great, they were jet-lagged and just starting to play as a team. Did they have a big conference to address this? Not quite. The hotel in Geneva was elegant but the elevators were a one-person deal (and considering the size of most of our junior players probably a tight squeeze) so the players used the stairs. If you happened to be a guest in the hotel you would have found yourself knee-deep in players one day when coach Mike Babcock and some of his players got to talking informally on the stairs.

Paiement remembers the players, including Larson, Dube and Denis all sitting in the stairwell discussing the team. He credits this informal session as a turning point for the team. Team building doesn't always fit neatly on the schedule but facilitating and encouraging it are an important part of the coach's job.

Doing Your Homework

Paiement puts the systems together in June. This effort comes after extensive consultation with former coaches. Paiement might be carrying the torch this year but that doesn't mean he is on his own. The national team has first-class coaching alumni and they are always ready to be a resource for the current coach. Top coaches like Tom Renney, Dave King, and Don Hay will always return phone calls.

Paiement subscribes to the motto "know the enemy." He has videos of the players he can expect to meet at the tournament and he reviews them carefully. You have to prepare to face European systems and styles. One of the things he needs to look at in selecting players is which players will be able to make the adjustment to a different style.

Canada vs. the World: Pressure?

Canada has history, five consecutive gold medals, and no one wants to break the streak. Paiement admits there is pressure but notes, "you can use pressure as an enemy or a friend and I have decided to use it as an ally." He sees the tournament as an opportunity for the coaching staff to show what they are made of. He admits that "every time you put the Maple Leaf jersey on you are expected to win." He did not ask the team to win Canada's sixth gold medal; he asked this team to win its first.

FINAL COMMENTS

The Game

Real Paiement: "I enjoy what I do and I think they (players) have to go to the rink and enjoy. This is the best game, the fastest game, the most demanding mentally and physically and it is great preparation for the real world, a competitive world."

The Job

Tom Renney: If your playing career is going down fast but you are still interested in coaching how do you know if you have what it takes? According to Renney technical knowledge is great but ultimately it is a gut thing. Like any job or profession, to do it and do it well you need to have some innate ability. Good coaches have a feel for the game and the players. Obviously Renney feels he has the instinct and his successes in coaching justify that belief.

If you're going to coach you have to have the guts to do things your way. Renney admits this can be dangerous to your job health but it is the only way to be a successful coach. When a team decides it is time to make a major change it is often easier to change the coach than the players.

In final analysis this is what Renney has to say: "I am doing my ultimate job—I like what I do. I help twenty-four people enjoy an experience like never before."

The Commitment

Parry Shockey: The players aren't the only ones who impress Shockey. He has a lot to say about the commitment of time and effort that parents make to allow their young children to play hockey. Credit where credit is due: you can't forget where players are first learning the game. "I get paid but I remember what it is like to be a parent/coach; you run into some really unique people." He was in Calgary recently and saw some young hockey players, maybe six or seven years old, out with a group of dads. He recognizes that without those volunteers the game would not be what it is. According to Shockey, "People who donate their time deserve a lot of respect."

Chapter 11
THE SEASON: A YEAR IN THE LEAGUE

SO YOU MADE THE TEAM and you are in great shape—what now? Well, brace yourself for a long, tough season. The CHL year starts early and if you're lucky enough to make it to the Memorial Cup Tournament, it ends late.

THE SEASON STARTS: THE REGULAR SEASON

Making the team means signing up for a long schedule of home and away games. The teams play close to seventy games during the regular season. The pressure of performing for so long can be very wearing on a young player.

A Player's Perspective: *Dylan Gyori, Tri-City Americans*

Dylan Gyori, a native of Red Deer, Alberta, shares his experiences playing with the Tri-City Americans. When he was sixteen Dylan joined the Tri-City Americans for his first season. He is now in his fourth year with the team. It has been an occasionally frustrating, often enjoyable three years for this young prospect.

1995-96—I Left Home for This?

When Dylan joined Tri-City he started out playing regularly but as the veterans returned from pro camps, the rookies spent more time on the bench. Of the fifty games that Dylan dressed for during his first year he estimates that he played in about half that number.

You do not move hundreds of miles away from home to sit on a bench. People kept saying he was learning, but Dylan is a learn-by-doing kind of guy. With the limited ice time he became frustrated. Dylan was accustomed to dominating the game, being the star, getting the glory; now he felt like a bencher.

Dylan Gyori, No. 19 – Tri-City Americans,
*Photograph courtesy of Jeff Fulks Photography and the
Tri-City Americans*

The lack of ice time was undermining Dylan's confidence. The team drafted him because he was a hot prospect; why weren't they playing him? He thought about returning home to play Midget. At least he would be playing. Dylan held off on returning home. He felt that at the very least he was paying his dues and would earn more ice time next season.

1996-97—A Disappointing Second Season

Dylan went back to Tri-City his second year hoping to have a better year. Actually he was hoping to have a really good year. He was draft-eligible and wanted to hear his name called in June. With nine players gone to the NHL and AHL there was lots of room on the ice. Unfortunately, after sitting on the bench so much the previous season the few ex-rookies remaining were a bit shaky. With twelve new rookies the team was looking for impact performances from their young prospects.

This shaky start to a high-pressure season was compounded by a personal loss. The woman who billeted Dylan during his first season died of cancer early in the new season. Although his teammates and team management were supportive Dylan was hit hard by the loss.

Despite media projections that he would go in the 1997 Entry Draft Dylan was overlooked and like any young player he was heartbroken. It was a miserable end to what had so far been a pretty unpleasant junior career.

As a third-year veteran of the league, Dylan could look back on those first two years and admit they were pretty horrible. A lot of the stress from those two seasons came from pressure Dylan put on himself, first to earn a spot on the team and then to get drafted to the NHL. If he had a chance to do it over again Dylan would ease up a bit, have some fun and take his nose off the skate grinder. Working hard is fine, but putting too much pressure on yourself can lead to burnout.

Dylan was pretty burned out by the end of his second season. For the first time he decided to get away from the rink. As a member of elite national teams Dylan usually played through the summer. He played on both the World Under-17 Team and the Under 18 National Team. Making the rosters of those teams was an impressive accomplishment but he was ready for a break.

1997-98 – Third Time Is the Charm

When the 1996-97 hockey season ended Dylan did what a lot of Canadian kids do—he got a job. He went to work lining pipe for his Dad. The job landed him in a work camp in Northern Alberta. The money was good and Dylan enjoyed having a break from hockey. With a job that went from sunrise to sunset he didn't have to worry about getting out of shape.

After a season that was tough physically and mentally Dylan was happy to have a chance to re-charge his batteries. He admits the thought occasionally hovered: should he give up? The thought was never a serious option for Dylan. He loved hockey too much and had worked too hard to get where he was.

Things did change for Dylan. He went into the 1997-98 season relaxed and re-focused. He had been overlooked in the NHL Draft but he was nowhere near finished chasing his dream of NHL stardom. This time he was determined to have some fun doing it. One of the biggest lessons he learned over his three years in the league is to relax a bit: "You cannot get too high or too low; you need to stay level-headed."

Without the pressure of the draft and having adjusted to the schedule, Dylan played well. He was more accustomed to sleeping at odd times and

Dylan Gyori
Canada Hockey
Photograph courtesy of the
Gyori family

traveling all over the West. In his third season Dylan was a first-line player who led his team in scoring, a performance that earned him a spot in the WHL's 1997 All-Star game.

He looked strong heading into the 1998 Entry Draft but he was not worried about it. Since his career didn't end when he was passed over in 1997, Dylan has learned to relax a bit. Dylan credits the summer he took off as being a renewal. He is having fun again and his game is improved.

The hard work and persistence have finally paid off for Dylan. People told him to relax and be patient when he was a rookie. They said ease up and have some fun his draft-eligible year. He did not listen but that is his advice to young players coming up. You have to really love the game and that means keeping your perspective and having fun.

Dylan realizes young players may not listen to him and he can understand that. Sometimes you have to learn from your own experiences. It is part of maturing and finding your comfort zone in a field that can be competitive and frustrating.

ROAD TRIPS: LIFE ON THE BUS

Road trips are a major part of life in the league. The Major Junior league is a traveling league with half of the regular season's games played on the road. Four players share their experiences with traveling in the league. Players comment that friends often think it is a glamorous part of the game, traveling to exotic destinations. Our players reveal that there is very little glamour in northern Alberta, northern Ontario or northern Quebec in winter.

The Prairies In Winter

Stephen Peat is a defenceman with the Red Deer Rebels and he has seen most of Western Canada and a few American states through the window of a bus during the season. The WHL is divided into three leagues with most of the games being played within the division, but every team plays together at least once. Teams will often do a circuit, visiting several teams on the road before returning home. The swing down to Spokane, Tri-City and Portland can mean spending twenty hours on the bus.

Dylan Gyori is back and forth across the U.S. border regularly during the year. As a member of the Tri-City Americans in Washington state he is often heading north to play. The longest trip he makes during the year is thirty-nine hours. Last year the team got a break from the road and hopped a plane to Prince George in northern B.C.

Boats, Buses and Planes—the Screaming Eagles See Quebec

Josh Dill of the new Cape Breton Screaming Eagles is familiar with bus trips, boat trips, and the occasional flight. Although Cape Breton is an enthusiastic home for the new team, being on the outskirts of the league means a lot of travel time. The team does take some short cuts. They frequently take the ferry to Quebec. That means bringing along Gravol; many of the players prefer their water frozen. Being on a ferry doesn't mean missing your nap. Players will often bring up their pillows and blankets and stretch out in a quiet corner of the lounge.

The team also flies to Montreal and plays several games against surrounding area teams before returning home to Cape Breton. Dill's advice to rookies when it comes to flying—don't throw your tickets away when you get there. Several of the Eagles tossed their tickets. Unfortunately they were round trip tickets. Dill was luckier than his teammates, he left his on the plane and it was waiting at the terminal. Most of the time all the travel means sleeping in whatever hotel you find yourself, but the Eagles did manage to squeeze in a game at the new Forum during one of their stops in Montreal.

Passing the Time

What do the players do to pass all those hours on the bus? The buses are equipped with televisions and the teams bring along videos. Pity the poor player sent to make the selection; he gets to spend the next twenty or so hours listening to complaints. According to Dill his team will often bring as many as fifteen videos along on a trip and by the end of the trip all the videos have been played. With French and English players you have to try get something for everyone. Well, almost everyone. Cape Breton video stores are short on Norwegian and Russian flicks.

Players often try to sleep on the long trips. Stephen Peat notes that after a Friday night game the team often showers, eats and gets on the bus to drive through to their next destination. The team tries to get there the day before to give players a chance to sleep in the hotel. Players are housed three to a room with the rookie getting the cot.

All three leagues share a common trait when it comes to the seating arrangements. Rookies start out in pairs in the front. The veterans get their own seats. Larry Paleczny of Owen Sound notes that players tend to stick to one seat during the whole season. Some players forgo their seats and stretch out on the floor. Dill doesn't endorse this practice but has teammates who prefer the floor to cramped quarters on the seat.

Tri-City's Dylan Gyori is one of the players who prefers stretching out even if it is on the floor. He does come prepared. Players who sleep on the floor bring sleeping bags, foams, and pillows. Some also bring earplugs to drown out the rumble from the bus. Sleeping on the floor is not a good thing if you are wearing a suit. Although the players wear suits to and from the game, when they are heading out on long trips they wear sweats or track suits.

Gameboy is a popular item during the long trips and some players read or do homework. Paleczny sees an advantage to bringing your school books. If you are having difficulties one of the other players has probably already taken the course and can give you some help. Despite high-tech gadgets, cards, games and just chatting are still popular ways to pass the long trips.

Larry Paleczny admits that the OHL has the shortest road trips but he does log some long hours on the bus when they head north to the Soo. He feels that road trips are a great time for team bonding. Players get a chance to get to know each other better.

Snack Time

Players need to eat on the road but that doesn't mean fast food. Athletes quickly realize the impact of diet on performance and shy away from greasy or high fat snacks. The teams regularly stop at convenience stores or restaurants for healthy snacks and meals. Dill notes that pasta and chicken are popular choices. If time is an issue the team picks up the meals and players eat on the bus.

THE PLAYOFFS: THE PUSH FOR THE POST SEASON

Despite the long regular season the real focus for players is the post season. A team practices all year for a chance to take it all the way to the league championships and onward to the Memorial Cup Tournament. Playoffs begin in mid-March for the CHL teams and culminate in a May tournament that pits the league champions and a host team against each other in a bid for the Cup.

Bryan Allen, Oshawa Generals

In his rookie season Bryan Allen joined a very focused bunch of players on the Oshawa Generals. The team was dominated by older players who were hoping to leave junior with a Memorial Cup ring and that meant winning the OHL championship. That desire translated into a hard-working team. Bryan credits the veterans with teaching him about drive and focus. Despite living in the shadow of the Ottawa 67's in the regular season, the team remained confident. That confidence translated into an unshakable desire to win.

Post-season play is the goal of every player but it makes for a long year. Prior to joining the Generals, Bryan's regular season was thirty-six games. He was coming off sixty games and heading into a playoff run. He did not even get a break at Christmas; Bryan was a member of the Under-17 national team and played during the Christmas holiday.

Despite some pretty tired moments his energy level was great during the playoffs. It is so important and so intense that you get a second wind. You need that second wind because the playoffs mean an intense schedule. The team usually played every second day or at least every third day. If the series goes the full seven games it makes for an exhausting run.

Holding Down Your Day Job

The playoffs do not mean players can step out of their regular lives. Bryan was in high school and had to carry his course load despite the playoff run. It was tough to keep up with everything. The fact that the team played in the league championship meant that Bryan finished out his academic year in Oshawa.

Getting a Breather

Bryan credits an unexpected bye with giving the team a chance to regroup. The bye should have gone to the Ottwa 67's but the team decided to pass and the Generals were the beneficiaries of that decision. The bye meant a break of ten days before the Generals started their first series. Bryan was made doubly aware of the importance of a rest when the team was catapulted into the Memorial Cup Tournament only two days after winning the league championship.

The Games

Injuries and a strong regular season performance allowed the rookie defenceman to earn a regular shift during the playoffs. The ten days the team had off allowed Bryan to catch his breath and start applying some of what he had learned. The regular season had taught him a lot and he brought that out in the playoffs. With a +6 plus/minus and four points during the playoffs he was a solid contributor.

The playoffs are a new level of competition. The game is faster and more intense. Players put everything they have into every game. The games are pretty physical but players are careful not to take penalties. No one wants to lose because he gave the other team a power play opportunity.

The OHL League Champions 1996-97

After a hard-fought series the OHL Championship was decided in overtime. The rink was packed to the rafters when they finally popped the game-winner into the net. Bryan was not on the ice when the buzzer sounded but he was out there a minute later. He and every other member of the team mauled the game-winning scorer. The overtime goal made the Generals the 1996-97 league champions. The fans went crazy; for the first time since 1990 the Generals had done it.

For the rookie defenceman the feeling was indescribable. It was the culmination of a year of intense focus and discipline. It made every long road trip, every loss, every bruise, every sacrifice worth it. For the older players, the win was years

Bryan Allen, No. 77
Oshawa Generals
Photograph courtesy of Ian Goodall

of work and building finally realized. Later, the team would be honored and take its place in the record books but for now the exhausted, sweat-soaked young players just reveled in the hard-won victory.

THE MEMORIAL CUP: MAJOR JUNIOR'S QUEST FOR THE CUP

When you are playing Major Junior and you talk about winning the cup, you aren't dreaming about an NHL future, you are planning an assault on the Holy Grail of the CHL— the Memorial Cup. This cup has a long and illustrious history in seventy-nine years as the coveted trophy of amateur hockey. The cup is a memorial to the many Canadian soldiers who sacrificed their lives in the First World War.

The cup actually pre-dates the modern-day Major Junior league. It began its existence as the Ontario Hockey Association (OHA) Memorial Cup. It was donated by the OHA to serve as the prize in a national junior competition. When Junior "A" and "B" hockey were carved out in 1934 the cup was awarded to the Canadian Junior "A" Champion. Further division took place in the 1960s when Junior was divided into Major Junior (Tier 1) and Junior "A" (Tier II). The cup went with the Major Junior league.

The first Memorial Cup Tournament was held in 1972 when the three leagues sent their league leaders to compete for the cup in a round-robin tournament. This week-long tournament culminated in a final sudden-death game between the two top teams. In 1983 the three league champion teams were joined by a fourth host team. The position as host and a bye into this tournament is rotated through all three leagues.

1995 Memorial Cup Tournament

Colin White's first shot at the Memorial Cup was in 1995. The Hull Olympiques led the league and earned a trip to Kamloops for the Memorial Cup Tournament. That year Hull was a bit of a Cinderella story. Colin was a freshman player and only played in one of the three games. It was not a good tournament for the team. Colin recalls, "We were so excited about going to the tournament—our focus was off. The

Oshawa Generals, – OHL Champions 1996-97
Photograph courtesy of Ian Goodall

weather was great, the hotel had an outdoor hot tub and the mood was—on vacation."

The Memorial Cup: a Player's Perspective

Memorial Cup 1997: Hull Olympiques

Colin does credit their poor showing with helping the team be more prepared for the 1997 tournament. Teams that earn a spot in the prestigious tournament may only find out a few days before the start. Hull knew they would be making a bid for the cup from the beginning of the season. Two advantages of hosting are more preparation time for the team, and family members and friends can arrange for tickets and accommodations.

The Hull Olympiques came first in the regular season, and picked up the QMJHL championship. As the host team, the Olympiques did not need to win the league championship for a berth but it was still important to the players. It also meant that despite a second place finish in the league Chicoutimi got a berth at the tournament.

Preparing for the Tournament

When Hull defeated Chicoutimi in the league playoffs, they earned some rest. The four-game sweep meant the team had ten days instead of four before the Memorial Cup tournament started. Despite being the home team and although they appreciated the crowds showering everyone with "Hull hospitality," the team packed up and headed for an undisclosed lodge outside the city. Team management wanted the team to stay together as a unit to strengthen their focus during the tournament. Colin emphasizes that "focus is so important" and "during the condensed time periods, mental toughness is critical."

Facing New Teams

During each Memorial Cup Tournament, the three leagues come together and that means facing new talent. The team had been scouting the OHL and WHL. Each player spent time reviewing videos of the teams they would be facing, getting to know the players and their styles. Colin noted this is something they did not do at Kamloops, and it helped this year. "We had a better sense of what you would be facing. Our team did not try to match the other teams. Our strategy was to play our game, roll our lines and let the others worry about matching us."

Playing To the Home Town Crowd

Another advantage of hosting is having the home crowd. Loyal fans had cheered for Hull all season and Colin felt that the team was less nervous. Colin's parents, grandparents and many special friends traveled from Nova Scotia to see him play. They worried that their presence might be an added pressure on Colin but he appreciated their being there. When the team won, with his family there, the experience was a shared one.

The stands are also choked with NHL scouts. Although Colin had already been drafted second round by the New Jersey Devils he still wanted to make a good showing. "Each game is so fast and intense that I don't think about the scouts when I am playing. When the game is over and I start to go over my performance, looking for weaknesses, assessing areas to improve on, I wonder what the scouts thought."

The Tournament

Hull started the tournament with an 8-0 win over the Oshawa Generals. Their second game began in the same form with a second period 6-0 lead on the Lethbridge Hurricanes. Despite the early lead, when the final buzzer rang the teams were stuck in a 6-6 tie. Lethbridge capped its comeback with an overtime goal. Colin felt the loss was good for the team. Early success seemed to make them over-confident. Lethbridge's come-from-behind victory made the team re-focus.

The Olympiques got a break during the tournament. When Hull and Lethbridge tied for games won and lost, the criteria became goals. Hull's victory over Oshawa gave them the points to earn a bye into the final game. This gave them a day off before the game and according to Colin, "We may have been a little less bruised and a little less tired." When they met the Hurricanes in the final game of the Tournament, the Hull Olympiques came away with the Cup.

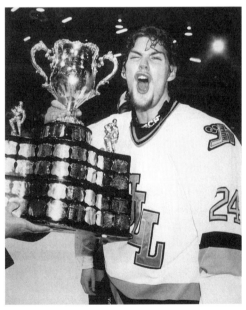

Colin White and the Memorial Cup
Photograph courtesy of the White family and Hull Olympiques

111

A Role Player Steps Up

Colin is not a Gretzky. He knows what he is and what he contributes to the team. He is a defensive defenceman. He saw frequent ice time, generating modest points and major penalty minutes during the regular season. Pressure seems to bring out the best in the young defenceman because his play stepped up during the playoffs and the tournament. This resulted in fifteen points in fourteen playoff games. His contributions continued with four points in four games at the Memorial Cup Tournament.

Colin White and Captain Steve Low celebrating the team's victory
Photograph courtesy of the White family and Hull Olympiques

The win was a huge achievement for the team and the city was right there to celebrate the win. A parade for the triumphant players was attended by fifty thousand fans. The Memorial Cup champions were invited to attend a Montreal Expos game. As guests of honour, the players were introduced individually on the ball field and then settled back to watch the game from the owner's box. The team only had a few days together before heading off for home and various training camps, but it was a great time.

On Winning the Cup

"To us, it was just like being in the NHL and trying to win the Stanley Cup. We wanted to have our names on that trophy. When I read the names from other years I am just so proud to be a part of the win. It's really something to know my name will be on the cup. The team will always be remembered."

Colin also wanted to include a sincere "Thank you" to his teammates, coaches and the people in Hull. The 1997 Memorial Cup win will definitely be the highlight of his junior career.

Chapter 12
COMMON INJURIES AND
COMMON SENSE

For SOME PLAYERS that long season is suddenly and painfully shortened. The high number of games and highly competitive play increases the risk of injuries. After all, despite precautions hockey is a contact sport. It's a physical game, rough, tough and hard-hitting. This chapter examines some of the most common injuries in hockey, the importance of proper treatment, and prevention.

CONCUSSIONS: A HIGH-PROFILE INJURY IN THE NHL

On May 2nd 1996 Brett Lindros was forced into retirement at age twenty, only two years after he began playing in the NHL. In a dream-breaking press conference the 6'3" right wing informed the world that he would no longer be playing for health reasons. The New York Islanders' first round draft choice in 1994 was sidelined after fifty-one games.

Other NHLers forced out of the game by concussions include Michel Goulet of the Chicago Blackhawks, Warren Babe of the Minnesota North Stars and Mike Eaves of the Calgary Flames. Michel Goulet was wearing a broomball helmet when his skate caught in a rut and he slammed head first into the boards. The impact put the player in a coma for a week and in therapy for a year.

More recently Mighty Ducks Paul Kariya missed the 1998 Olympics due to a concussion and Pat LaFontaine had his season with the Rangers shortened after a collision with a team member. He has since retired from the game. It is difficult to hide bruises, sprains and breaks. It is easier to appear to shake off head injuries that don't show external physical symptoms and keep playing but they have the potential for a devastating impact on the young player's future.

113

If you are getting the message that concussions are dangerous you may be wondering what exactly they are.

What is a Concussion?

"Getting Your Bell Rung"

Players have the attitude that despite getting their "bell rung" they can get right back in the game. Many people are under the impression a concussion must involve loss of consciousness or some other severe neurological symptoms. This is a misconception that Ottawa Senators team doctor Jamie Kissick would like to correct. The sports world is slowly waking up to the seriousness of this injury.

Concussion = Mild Traumatic Brain Injury

When it comes to understanding concussions Dr. Kissick prefers a more helpful term—mild traumatic brain injury. Dr. Kissick indicates that a traumatic brain injury is "any traumatically-induced injury that causes an alteration of brain function." What this means is the impact of the brain hitting the inside of the skull when you hit your head or when you have an explosive movement that causes your brain to slide into your skull.

Some signs of a traumatic brain injury are loss of consciousness, blurred vision, confusion, feeling "dazed" or "woozy," amnesia about the event, headache, loss of balance, ringing in the ears or nausea. When trainers or health professionals suspect a concussion they ask questions that the player should be able to answer.

One player remembers being asked where he was after a hit and naming an arena that the team played the previous week. Another player remembers a teammate repeatedly asking the same question despite being told the answer several times. Though he had not been knocked unconscious, one player was extremely nauseous after hitting his head. These types of responses indicate that a concussion has occurred.

How Do I Know If I Have One?

Unfortunately, this injury may not be easy to recognize. One young defenceman thought that he had never had a concussion; he had never been knocked unconscious. He did admit to being hit hard enough to produce confusion. About fifteen minutes later, when he could see the scoreboard again, he got right back in the game. Unconsciousness is a sign of a traumatic brain injury but it is not a necessary sign.

It is critical for players to make an effort, after a blow to the head or a body blow that jars the head, to carefully assess their condition. Even

114

very serious concussions can result in confusion only. According to Dr. Kissick there is an increasing awareness that repeated concussions, even small ones, can result in permanent functional impairment.

Dr. Kissick has an advantage in assessing impact injuries for his players. He can check the replay to get a clear picture of the hit and the immediate reaction. This isn't available at most levels of the sport. But the biggest advantage Dr. Kissick has is the highly-qualified athletic therapists or trainers who assess the player immediately and can identify the initial symptoms. This assists the doctor in providing guidance to help players assess their condition after receiving a traumatically-induced head injury.

Initial Assessment: Some Tips In Assessing the Injury

The first advice that Kissick gives is always to err on the side of caution. Concussions are dangerous. Keep the player out of the game and get a professional assessment. Some advice that may help with identifying and assessing a mild traumatic brain injury is to test the player's orientation, concentration and memory. What does that mean in practical terms? Dr. Kissick offers some basics.

Ask the player how he feels, ask about physical symptoms, get a detailed response. How is his vision? Any nausea, disorientation, dizziness?

Ask if the player remembers the hit, the shift, the events immediately prior to the incident. Amnesia about the event is one of the factors in the two main guidelines for diagnosing and treating concussions.

Check the player's memory and concentration:
- ask questions about current events
- ask the player what team he played against last week
- tell the player three items and then wait for a bit and ask him to repeat the items
- ask the player to count backward from one hundred by sevens to check concentration

These suggestions provide some guidance in assessing a player immediately after a hit. They are not a substitute for prompt medical attention. The questions and responses, and the initial impressions, should be conveyed to the treating physician. This will help the doctor to assess and classify the concussion.

What should be clear is that a "Yeah, Coach, I'm fine" is not going to cut it. Ignored injuries can come back to haunt players. One of Dr. Kissick's biggest frustrations is seeing young players coming in with poorly-managed concussions.

What Do You Do When You Have One?
When you tear a ligament or sprain a limb you sit out. A mild traumatic brain injury may not carry obvious debilitating physical symptoms but it is still important to give yourself time to heal. There is a period of time after each concussion when the brain is vulnerable to further injury. Second injuries are especially likely during this time period for two reasons.

The first reason is that seemingly trivial confusion means an athlete's protective reflexes may not be working well and he may be unable to avoid taking hits in a fast rugged game.

The second reason is that when a player has an unhealed concussion "the brain is not fully reconnected" and a small hit can result in very serious damage. This **second impact syndrome** causes swelling in the brain. This condition is extremely rare but can have lethal consequences.

How Do You Know When You Are In This Vulnerable Condition?
Players may have headaches, trouble concentrating or may just "not feel right." The length of the healing period varies and it is best determined by a physician. Players should always be cleared by a doctor before they return to the game. Your gray matter is still a bit of a gray area within the medical profession. There is an extraordinary amount of research being undertaken by doctors in the field of sports medicine to better understand these injuries.

The necessary healing period is determined on a case-by-case basis. Again Kissick advises to err on the side of caution and give yourself the time you need to heal. There are a number of guidelines that provide a formula for determining how long a player should wait before returning to play.

The New OHA Guidelines Developed By OBIA
The Ontario Brain Injuries Association (OBIA) has recently come forward to provide some guidance in the treatment of concussions. OBIA has developed a new set of guidelines for the OHA to help the league manage concussions. According to Executive Director Dr. Barry Willer, the guidelines do not provide a revolutionary new way to treat concussions; giving the player time to heal is still the only way. The

guidelines provide some assistance in determining when players can get back in the game.

Concussions are divided into three grades and appropriate management depends on properly categorizing the injury. To properly classify the concussion the doctor will look at the nature and the duration of the symptoms. In all cases after receiving a concussion the player should be removed from the game and should not be returned to play unless cleared by a physician.

Second and repeated concussions are considered to be very serious and the player will be required to stay out of the game for a longer period of time. The decision about when a player can return to play will be made by the treating physician.

Speaking Up

Since a determination that a player is completely without symptoms is a critical first step, careful assessment by the player and honest responses are essential. It may seem very important to get back to the game as quickly as possible but if you want to stay in the game you have to be properly healed.

Dr. Willer is quick to point out that the treating physician is not at the mercy of the player's response. There are tests that help determine if a player is ready to be cleared. An example is putting a player on a treadmill and having him count backwards from one hundred by sevens. This tests the players concentration under physical stress. This is extremely important because symptoms that may have seemed to disappear may return when the player is under physical stress.

Post-Concussion Syndrome

When NHL players are on the injury list you hear the term "post-concussion syndrome." You know the origin of the injury, but what is the syndrome? According to Dr. Kissick the phrase is a bit of a catch-all. The syndrome has various symptoms including headaches, personality changes, mood swings and various neurological symptoms including memory loss and impaired concentration.

On a Personal Level

Concussions are serious and have a very real impact on a player's life. Players have expressed frustration and embarrassment in dealing with this medical condition.

The frustration comes from dealing with symptoms that have no real treatment except time. Elite young athletes suddenly face weaknesses and symptoms that can be difficult to deal with. Forgetting how to do simple tasks, not doing well at school because you cannot concentrate, and mood swings can leave a player feeling vulnerable and scared.

Behavioural changes are a particularly difficult symptom of concussions. Players may experience a change in personality that makes life difficult for friends and family members. Players may demonstrate symptoms including irritability, aggressive behaviour, anger and depression. A player may have an emotional response to a situation that is completely out of proportion to the incident. It is important to recognize that behavioural changes are as much a symptom of the concussion as headaches or memory loss.

There may not be a bruise or any other physical sign of the injury but post-concussion syndrome is real. Players can end up feeling embarrassed by having a serious medical condition which may have no physical signs. People who are ignorant about brain injuries may express doubts as to the seriousness or even the existence of the injury. The player can look perfectly healthy but the injury is extremely serious. Increased awareness of the condition in the sports industry has helped address this by providing education and support for athletes and their families.

Neuropsychological Testing: a New NHL Policy

One of the biggest difficulties in assessing and treating traumatic brain injuries is the lack of empirical evidence. A concussion does not change colour like a bruise, you cannot see the bones knit on the X ray or the swelling go down. What the NHL has done to help identify the effects of the injuries is to start baseline neuropsychological testing.

When a player shows up at training camp he will be tested. The test provides a measure of the player's mental acuity. The results of this test give doctors a tool to assess the player's injuries. By comparing the results of the test after an injury to the pre-injury results, doctors get an indication of changes in brain function.

This test is a tool and not the sole factor in determining when a player is ready to get back on the ice. It is part of the NHL's attempts to gauge the impact of the injury and ensure that players are fully healed before they are cleared to play.

OCULAR (EYE) INJURIES

Players in the CHL are required to wear visors. Their NHL counterparts are not. In a game at Maple Leaf Gardens, Teemu Selanne scored, not an unusual occurrence for the young star but in this case it was an unusual goal. The puck ricocheted off his visor and into the net. Fortunately, he was wearing a visor at the time. There is a tendency for players to stop wearing their visors when they move into the NHL.

Dr. Tom Pashby is an expert on ocular injuries. He is also the recipient of the Order of Canada for his work in hockey safety. In addition to being the driving force behind the introduction of visors and masks to the game, he continues to research the causes and types of ocular injuries occurring in sports.

His research reveals the seriousness of ocular injuries. A total of 1,759 eye injuries including 271 blind eyes have occurred in eighteen seasons between 1972 and 1991. Even the injuries that did not result in blindness were serious enough to require ophthalmological care.

As with any injury, prompt treatment is a must. If a player receives an eye injury he should seek prompt attention from an ophthalmologist. Even for non-organized play Dr. Pashby recommends that there be at least one person present trained in first aid and able to assess injuries.

There are two avenues of attack in protecting players from sports injuries: the equipment that players wear and the rules of the game.

LEAGUE POLICY

Unfortunately the NHL does not mandate that players wear Canadian Standards Association (CSA)-approved helmets or visors. Fortunately the CHL league does not follow the big leagues on this issue and requires that its players wear CSA-approved helmets and visors.

In addition to ensuring the helmets lined up on the bench are regulation, the league has also taken steps to ensure that the players are always wearing those helmets when they are on the ice. The OHL tightened its helmet policy in the 1996-97 season. Now, when a player loses his helmet, he is required to retrieve it immediately or get off the ice.

The WHL has a similar policy, with a ten-minute penalty assessed to players who fail to retrieve their headgear. Referees are also instructed to ensure that the players are wearing the chin strap properly. When worn tight against the chin, the strap will keep the helmet in place when it is jarred. The league has also introduced the requirement that players wear mouthguards.

No Dah: Why Don't Players Wear Their Helmets Properly?

If you've already read the section on concussions and ocular injuries you are probably wondering why hockey players don't wear proper headgear. Players cite all sorts of reasons. The big ones are vanity and comfort. Strapping on a helmet may not be the most comfortable thing in the world but smart players are going to protect their brains.

You see it all the time: a player with a chin strap dangling loosely from the helmet. This allows the players to push the visor that is supposed to be protecting his eyes up onto his forehead. Unfortunately it also allows the helmet to be knocked off. One young player admits this is exactly what happened to him. He was knocked unconscious when he and his helmet hit the ice separately. He was out cold for about five minutes and out of the game for a month until he was cleared to play again.

Players are learning to protect their heads. When Bryan Marchment, wearing a field hockey helmet, stopped convulsing after he hit the boards in a 1997 playoff game he strapped a regulation CSA-approved helmet on before taking to the ice again. When it comes to proper wear, New York Rangers Pat LaFontaine is a role model. LaFontaine returned to the game with a tightly-cinched chin strap. This keeps his helmet in place and maximizes the protection offered by his equipment.

PLAYING THE GAME: EDUCATING THE PLAYER

The league is making an effort to ensure that young players are learning proper techniques before taking to the ice. Improperly executed checks and illegal hits have the potential to cause serious damage to players. In an effort to ensure that players are learning the right way to play hockey the Canadian Hockey Association (CHA) produces videos on a variety of aspects of the game.

Many of the tapes are targeted at technical skills and all include cautions on the importance of proper technique. These videos are available to players of all ages from Atom to Major Junior. The CHA publishes a resource catalogue that allows coaches to order these videos.

According to Rob Cookson of the CHA, a video called *The Respect Effect* is aimed at ensuring that the game is played responsibly and with the recognition that hockey is a vigorous physical sport. Playing safely means playing properly and with respect for other players.

The video is a group effort. It was made with the support and expertise of the Canadian Academy of Sports Medicine, whose hockey safety committee was a driving force in the production of the video.

Mr. Cookson says it is designed to focus on more than just hockey and he hopes that young players will learn to carry over the principles into everyday life. These videos are a non-profit endeavor by the CHA to ensure the best possible education for young players.

BELOW THE NECK: COMMON SPORTS INJURIES

The head is not the only body part at risk of injury. In a physical sport like hockey, other injuries, from bruises to breaks, are common. Dave Wright is an athletic therapist with The Sports Medicine Specialists Clinic in Toronto. The clinic is owned by Dr. Michael Clarfield and Dr. Darrell Ogilvie-Harris, the team doctors for the Toronto Maple Leafs.

Wright is one of the seven athletic therapists working at the clinic. The clinic deals with a variety of sports injuries, and in addition to the athletic therapists, also employs seven physiotherapists. They focus on complete treatment, from injury to return to play. The goal is to send the player back rehabilitated and stronger than pre-injury.

Wright's interest in the medical side of sports came as a result of his own experiences. When he was playing hockey he was hit from behind and received a neck injury. The injury gave Wright an up-close and personal look at treatment and rehab. Wright became certified as an athletic therapist in 1989 and continues to attend seminars in the rapidly evolving world of sports therapy.

Although the clinic serves athletes in many different sports, Wright has a special affinity for hockey. Wright is currently completing his Level Six as a referee with the CHA. He started out as a linesman with the OHL in 1989 and has since been promoted.

Wright shares his expertise in recognizing, treating and preventing some of the most common hockey-related injuries. Most injuries are the result of overuse or traumatic (impact) injuries. They also tend to occur more frequently in certain body parts. Knees, backs, and shoulders are the common sites for injuries.

The helpful tips in the following segment are not intended to be a substitute for prompt professional assessment and treatment.

Knees

Knees are designed to go in two directions and are vulnerable to injury when moved in any other direction. Stiff penalties are decreasing the number of knee-to-knee impact injuries but impact and overuse injuries are still common.

The most common injuries are sprains. Sprains occur when the limb is forced out of its usual location and the ligaments and tendons are

121

stretched to the point of tearing. There are three degrees of sprains. A first-degree sprain is very mild and involves micro tearing. What that means in "ouch terms" is some swelling and soreness. A second-degree sprain involves moderate tearing and can keep a player out from three to six weeks. A player may require an X ray and medication. A third-degree tear is a complete rupture and requires a doctor's attention and possible surgical repair.

Sprains and PIER : Pressure, Ice, Elevate, Rest

No matter which limb is affected, the treatment for mild sprains remains the same. If you receive a first-degree sprain prompt action can help minimize the effect of the injury. The acronym PIER provides guidance on dealing with sprains. It doesn't give the right order but IERP is not a word.

The first thing to do is ice the injury. That is ice, NOT heat. Heat dilates the blood vessels and increases the blood flow, causing the injury to swell more. A word of caution—longer is not better. An injury should be iced for no longer than twenty minutes. Any longer and your body starts thinking it is in trouble and makes an extra effort to heat the area. The standard practice is twenty minutes on and twenty minutes off. Ice can be reapplied three to five times per day for the first three days following the injury.

Elevating the injury also helps reduce the swelling by decreasing the flow of blood to the injured limb. Rest is critical. When you have an injury your body is weakened and more vulnerable. Stay away from weight bearing immediately after an injury. In layman's terms—don't run around on a sprain. Pressure usually takes the form of a bandage or a wrap that provides some support, compression and protection for the damaged limb while it heals.

You may think you are tough and can play through the pain. Try thinking of it this way: aggravating injuries just means you are playing your way into more pain. A fully recovered, healthy body is the best tool to bring to a sport.

After three days a player can do some mild stretching and range of motion exercises. This keeps the recovering limb mobile. When a player has full range of motion, full strength, no swelling and no pain, it's time to get back in the game.

Back Injuries

Anyone who watches pro hockey is aware that players frequently lose time to back injuries. Wright notes that he is seeing more postural dysfunction and lack of specific flexibility. It seems two common pieces of parental advice, "Sit up straight" and "If you keep doing that you'll freeze that way" are actually on target.

To help a player avoid these problems, Wright stresses the importance of proper stretching. Working out the upper back and not stretching properly can result in bigger but tighter muscles. Muscles will contract better when they are stretched. Often when players work out they overlook certain key body parts. Wright sums up the problem as "working what you see." Bulging biceps and a sculpted chest look good but will not stabilize your trunk and protect your lower back.

In addition to strengthening the lower back players need to do abdominal work. Trunk and abdominal strength, and pelvic stability are essential for hockey players to prevent mechanical injuries. Players who want function and not just form will ensure that they perform a balanced workout.

Stretching tips

Stretching is a key component of game preparation. Players often suit up and hit the ice for a warmup skate without properly stretching. The game is intense and players who are not properly warmed up risk muscle pulls and strains.

A proper stretch is static—that means no bouncing. The stretch should be up to the point of pulling, not to the point of pain. The stretch should be held for at least twenty seconds. If you are short on time, it is more effective to hold the stretch longer and do fewer repetitions.

Wright recommends investing in a good book on stretches or asking an athletic therapist or team trainer for some guidance. Every player should stretch his back, hips and legs before a game. The lower back is particularly important and often overlooked. This will help prevent muscle spasms and strains.

Shoulders

If you regularly play or attend hockey games the thud of players hitting the boards is a familiar sound. That impact can result in shoulder injuries. The most common form of injury is a sprain. The treatment of the injury will depend on which degree of sprain the player has received. First degree sprains need ice, pressure and rest but because of the location of the injury elevating is not feasible. A player may require a sling while he is recuperating from a shoulder injury.

Unlike knees, shoulders can be protected by equipment. Wright recommends using a donut pad inside the shoulder pad. This ring-shaped piece of foam will diffuse the force of the impact. Shoulder pads should also be chosen to maximize the player's protection. The gear should be snug but comfortable. Loose-fitting shoulder pads allow for slippage and decrease protection in a crunch. Shoulders need to move but shoulder pads should not.

Groin Injuries

If you keep track of NHL injuries you will note a number of players missing games to recuperate from groin pulls. According to Wright this type of injury has been increasing. It is not completely understood what causes these injuries. Wright suggests that softer ice forces players to dig in more deeply to achieve speed. This causes more thrust from the muscle and increases susceptibility to pulls and sprains. Blame can also be placed on poor groin flexibility and weak abdominals.

Some players try to ignore the warning tightness and twinges in the groin. Wright recommends that players pay serious attention to their bodies—the first pull that "doesn't feel quite right," soreness or irritation should get serious attention. Pain is a warning and players who ignore it may find the injury progressing to become a hernia. A hernia occurs when a piece of your intestine or other internal organ slides through a weak muscle wall and gets trapped.

Icing the injury and resting are the two most important steps a player can take to treat this injury. Players can also wrap the area to provide some added support while they are healing. A strong flexible muscle is less prone to injuries. While quads, calves, and hamstrings may receive regular strengthening and stretching, the inner thigh is often overlooked. Basic side leg raises will help strengthen this important part of a player's anatomy.

Forearms

Short gloves have become a fashion trend but they leave the player's forearms unprotected. Anyone who has had a stick across the forearm knows how important that protection is. There is little muscle and lots of bone in the forearm and fractures or breaks can occur. Long cuff gloves offer coverage to this vulnerable area. Wright has seen some players use slash pads to protect forearms from bruises and bone fractures.

Players' Perspectives: Life On the Injured List

Playing and practicing is a big part of a young hockey player's life. What happens when he is suddenly sidelined by an injury? Players admit it is extremely difficult. Injuries have a psychological impact.

Hockey is a team sport and players who are injured may find themselves isolated. It is not intentional but players who are injured cannot play and do not travel with the team. Whether the team is winning or losing, it is frustrating not to be able to contribute. Hockey is a huge part of the player's life and a player who is sidelined is often at loose ends. One player notes that you end up sitting around waiting to heal and trying not to lose your conditioning.

Timing can also add stress to being injured. A player who was injured during his draft-eligible season admits you worry about how it will affect your draft chances. Players sometimes try to keep playing. One player kept trying to play with a groin injury until it got so bad he could not take a full stride. He ended up out of the game for two weeks.

As frustrating and depressing as being injured can be, players should focus on the long term. Ignoring an injury can aggravate it and you end up rehabbing for an even longer time. It is difficult but important to stay positive and be patient.

Listening To Your Body

A common thread running through this segment is early identification and prompt treatment. Wright is adamant—no pain, no gain does not apply to injuries. Pain is your body's way of letting you know something is not right. Listen to it. Parents need to listen carefully to their kids. Recognizing pain and seeking treatment is not "whining." It is an important part of an athlete's body awareness.

Chapter 13
SOMETHING A LITTLE EXTRA: ANNUAL HIGHLIGHTS

PART OF THE ATTRACTION of the CHL is the exposure players receive. In addition to the regular season, the playoffs and the Memorial Cup, some fortunate players have additional commitments. During the year there are many special events and tournaments that feature top CHL players. Included in these are the Under-18 National Team, the World Junior Cup, the CHL Prospects Game and NHL Training camps.

REPRESENTING CANADA: INTERNATIONAL TOURNAMENTS

The World Junior Tournament

Every year since 1977 hockey-playing countries send their best young talent to the I.I.H.F.'s World Junior Championship held in December. The location of the tournament is rotated every year. Canada has hosted the tournament four times. Canada's National Junior Team has earned ten gold, two silver and two bronze medals in the tournament's twenty-three-year history.

Some of Canada's best hockey players have played for this team and every year twenty-two players have a chance to put on the Canadian jersey. Spots on this roster are coveted but only forty players are invited to the August selection camp. The first half of the season is a continuous audition for young players.

In December, thirty-two players are invited to the final selection camp. With only twenty-two slots on the roster and a few weeks to get ready to take on the world, it is a high-pressure time for the player. Final decisions are not made until the morning the team is scheduled to leave for the tournament.

A Player's Perspective: *Jesse Wallin, Red Deer Rebels*

Red Deer Rebels' defenceman Jesse Wallin has donned the Team Canada jersey twice. He was a member of both the 1996 and 1997 National Junior Teams. This first round draft pick of the Detroit Red Wings was deeply honoured by the chance to represent his country in the prestigious international event.

Jesse admits to being extremely nervous the first time he was invited to camp. He knew most of the players at the camp, if only by reputation. Jesse had no trouble motivating himself to train during the summer prior to the tournament. The invitation was a tremendous honour for the young player and he wanted to make sure he was in top form.

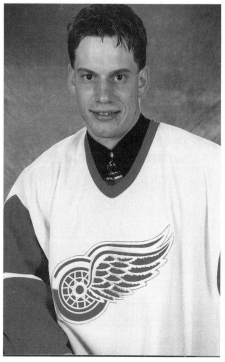

Jesse Wallin
Detroit Red Wings Prospect
Photograph courtesy of the CHL

The invitees went to the University of Calgary for the August camp. With the students off enjoying the summer, the young hopefuls settled into the dorms and got ready to perform. Although he did not know it that first summer, after two years in the program Jesse feels he has a sense of what the coaching staff is looking for at the summer camp.

Jesse feels they are looking for character, checking to see who is arriving in shape and ready to work hard. After the off-season, hockey senses are off, even for players in top condition, so it makes for some rusty performances at camp.

Jesse was invited back to the December camp and he was worried it would be tough. Despite a strong performance during the fall, he had been off for a couple of games with a badly bruised arm. There is a rhythm to the game and even the few games he missed were enough to worry the young defenceman. Competition would be tough and he could not afford to be a little bit off. He wasn't.

When it comes to playing with new teammates, it is something that he has faced before. Elite players move around a lot in their careers and new teammates are common. Jesse knows you need to do some quick bonding. The team has to get motivated and be operating smoothly in only a couple of weeks.

Jesse did not know if he was going to make the 1996 National Junior team. He kept working hard but he stuck to his style. Some players try to do more at camp, play a little differently. Jesse figured they brought him to camp because of the way he played so he stuck to it. Learning your role and doing it well is an important part of contributing to the team.

During the last exhibition game at camp Jesse was sat out. He was pretty worried about what that decision meant and it must have showed. The head scout, Barry Trapp, told him to relax. Jesse thought that was a good sign; at least he hoped it was.

The decision on the final roster is made during the night and the team leaves for the tournament the next day. Players who do not make the team are woken up early and flown home. It makes for a pretty restless night as players wait for the ominous footsteps in the hall and the knock on the door.

A player knows when he wakes up that he has made the team. He finds out whom he will be playing with at breakfast. It is a pretty excited group meeting over orange juice in the morning.

The team has a practice after breakfast and then goes to be outfitted. Jesse admits that getting your apparel is a big thing; it makes it "kind of official." The team then heads down for photos and TSN promotion shots.

The day is full but very exciting. Players call parents and friends to share the big news. Jesse's mom was very excited; she and his billet family made the trip overseas to catch the tournament. Jesse's father, Brian, died in 1994 and he privately dedicated the 1996 World Junior Championship to his dad.

The team attended a send-off dinner hosted by the NHLPA. The dinner included some inspirational moments courtesy of former members of Canada's National Teams. These former players shared their experiences representing Canada and the responsibility that goes with the honour.

The travel is tiring and players have to adjust quickly to the time difference. The team arrived in Geneva, Switzerland at 8:30 a.m. and went right to the rink. To help the players adjust to the time difference the team had to stay awake and reasonably coherent until the evening.

Jesse admits it was tough and there were some nodding heads at the practice.

The team arrived in Europe five days before the tournament started. They had some exhibition games to warm them up before the actual event. The first time you get a look at the ice you feel disoriented. The larger ice surface is a big adjustment. Jesse notes that it is more than just the size of the ice; the style of the game is also different. Europeans tend to play a less physical game so you know every guy out there is a good skater and puck handler.

Once the tournament started, the team got into a routine. With seven games in nine nights the tournament is a densely-packed experience. Players got up in the morning and met for breakfast; after eating they had some time off before the scheduled team event. Usually it was a team walk. It was not overly-demanding but it woke the players up.

After the walk the team was on its own. Jesse liked to hang out, maybe play cards with some teammates. The common areas in the hotel were often the site of impromptu card games. Some players slept and others wandered around and did some shopping. With so many games in such a short period, they kept it pretty quiet.

The tight game schedule did not leave much time for practices. Around two p.m. the team would have a pre-game meal and pre-game warmup. The hotel was accommodating in preparing the teams' meals so the players did not really have to make an adjustment for foreign food.

Players usually grabbed a quick nap after the warmup until four-thirty. Then the team would meet for a light snack and a motivational video. The video was a collection of Canadian moments from prior tournaments set to Tina Turner's "Simply the Best." Jesse admits it was pretty cool to see the highlights from his 1996 win in the video at the 1997 Tournament. After watching the video, pumped up, they would head for the rink. They usually blasted their theme song, "Simply the Best," while they stretched and warmed up.

That gold medal game was an intense experience. The team was playing for their country and trying to uphold a tradition of gold. When the final buzzer sounded the team piled up on the ice and according to Jesse it was absolutely incredible. All the players and the coaches were elated. Many of the players had family members and friends in the stands cheering for them.

The players received their medals, Canada's fifth consecutive gold, and the Canadian flag was raised. The team all helped out in singing the anthem. It was a very emotional moment. Jesse reflects that winning a gold medal is the sort of thing you dream about doing when you are a kid and to actually be part of it was just indescribable.

World Junior Tournament, 1997

The fact that he already had a gold medal from the 1996 World Junior Tournament did not detract from Jesse's disappointment at the 1997 Tournament when the team fell out of medal contention. As team captain he really wanted to step up and be a leader. An injury sidelined him halfway through the tournament.

It was very frustrating to have to watch from the sidelines as the team struggled. Jesse admits the loss was difficult for the team. Nobody came there to lose but it happened. Jesse stresses that losing is something that you have to learn to deal with as a player; obviously it is not anybody's favourite part of the sport but it is unavoidable. For Jesse, dealing with a loss means trying to learn from the experience, improve what you can and, most importantly, get on with your game.

Jesse Wallin, No. 4 – World Junior Tournament
Photograph courtesy of Dan Hamilton, Vantage Point Studios

The Under-18 Tri-Nations Tournament

Canada's National program also has an Under-18 team that represents our country on the world stage. Not as high profile as the World Junior Tournament team, the Under-18 Tournament offers players under the age of eighteen the opportunity to represent Canada. In 1997, the tournament was a Tri-Nations tournament in the Czech Republic.

Players were selected for the August tournament on the basis of their performance during the season. National team scout Barry Trapp explains that the lack of a selection camp is due to budget constraints and is something he is hoping will change. The tournament is an excellent way for young players to get international exposure and is often helpful in identifying players for the World Junior Cup team.

A Player's Perspective: *Stephen Peat, Red Deer Rebels*

Stephen Peat of the Red Deer Rebels was one of the players who received an invitation to don a Team Canada jersey and represent his country. Peat was thrilled by the invitation. It was a welcome and unexpected surprise for the young defenceman. Although there is no selection camp the team does have a training camp before heading off to Europe.

The week-long tournament was originally scheduled to be held in Prague but flooding in the city forced the games to be held in rinks in surrounding communities. Unlike their North American counterparts the rinks did not use artificial light. Instead large windows provided natural light.

The biggest adjustment was the larger ice surface. Peat admits it is an intimidating sight but you have to just get out there and play. The team defended Canada's position as a dominant force in hockey and brought home the gold.

Peat knows there was more than just the game to adjust to in an international tournament. The food was very different; most of the Canadian team lost weight during the tournament. There was a McDonald's but the team made only two trips during their stint.

Although the team did not really meet the players from other teams, Peat enjoyed getting to know his teammates. The team had players from all three junior leagues allowing Peat to meet players from other parts of Canada.

THE CHRYSLER CUP TOP PROSPECTS CHALLENGE

One way that the league provides exposure for draft-eligible players is the annual CHL Top Prospects Challenge. The Chrysler

Cup challenge took on its present form in 1995 when the CHL and NHL teamed up to make a prospects game. In its original format the game was a challenge between a host league all-star team and a combined all-star team from the two challenging leagues. The players for the game are now the top forty draft-eligible prospects in the CHL as determined by NHL central scouting.

The new game format featured new coaches, Bobby Orr vs. Don Cherry in a battle of prospect supremacy. This important game attracts quite an audience as scouts and GMs pack the stands to see what will be available in the June Entry Draft.

How important is this one game? According to Dan Marr, former Scouting Coordinator for the Toronto Maple Leafs, pretty important. These prospects are projected to be the cream of the league. The game gives scouts get a chance to see how players adjust to playing against the best in their draft group. Two hundred scouts packed the stands for the 1997 Prospects game; it looks like Marr's opinion is widely shared.

Playing In the Big Game: Players' Perspectives On the Prospects Game

Craig Hillier, Ottawa 67's, 1996

The first time the new format was adopted was in 1996. Rated as the number one goalie for the upcoming draft, Ottawa 67's netminder Craig Hiller was a sure bet to be making an appearance. Craig got the official word in January that he would be heading to Maple Leaf Gardens for the big event.

The game would be carried by TSN, giving family and friends back home in Nova Scotia the opportunity to watch the young prospect. They would not be the only people watching the game; Craig expected the game would be heavily scouted. It was a great opportunity for scouts to get a look at the 1996 prospects.

The players arrived in Toronto on Monday night, giving them some time to prepare for the Thursday night game. The first step was to create the teams. The first year the players were selected by means of a draft held at the Hockey Hall of Fame. Coaches Orr and Cherry flipped a coin to determine who would draft first. Cherry won the toss and decided to select the defence. Hillier was picked to backstop the team.

After the team was sorted out, the new teammates had some time to practice together before the big event. Craig said it was great having Cherry for a coach. He was really involved in the game. It was interesting to see the other top-rated prospects. Usually players only got a chance to see the guys in their own league. Craig got a chance to see number-one-rated prospect Chris Phillips but was more concerned with the performance of the other goaltenders. Craig was the only OHL netminder in the lineup.

In addition to the big game, the prospects also got to prove themselves at a skills competition. The players spent some time with underprivileged kids during the week. The week was high pressure but the guys managed to squeeze in some down time. They went to the mall and checked out the Hockey Hall of Fame. The high-profile game attracted lots of media attention; Craig did a number of interviews before the game.

With the eyes of the hockey world focused on the game, Craig was both excited and nervous. A player's performance can either help or hurt his draft position. The format meant that he would only get to play for half the game. Team Cherry's other goalie, Francis Larivee, would get equal time in nets.

Craig got to start the game. He admits he preferred to go in first. It gave him a chance to warm up. With eighteen shots on net Craig held Team Orr scoreless during his tenure between the pipes. It was an excellent performance and solidified Craig's position in the upcoming draft. He was the first goalie selected in the 1996 Entry Draft. When the dust settled, Team Cherry had a nine to three victory over Team Orr.

Jeff Zehr, Erie Otters, 1997

Jeff Zehr got the news that he had a spot on the Top Prospects roster one month before the game was scheduled to take place. He was ecstatic to say the least. Jeff knew the game was an important showcase for draft-eligible players.

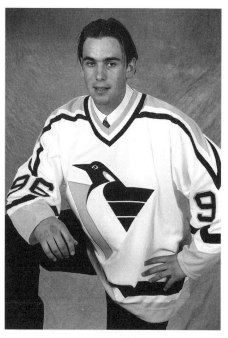

Craig Hillier
Pittsburg Penguins draft selection
Photograph courtesy the CHL and Dan Hamilton, Vantage Point Studios

For such an important game there was not a lot of preparation time. Jeff arrived in Toronto two days before the game. He was paired up at the hotel with Brendan Morrow. The scouts divided the players into two teams, Team Cherry and Team Orr. Players would be proud to call either one Coach. Jeff was slotted to play for Team Orr.

They did a bit of sight-seeing during their brief visit, featuring a trip to the Hockey Hall of Fame. There was considerable media attention surrounding the game and players had pictures and interview sessions. Jeff's favourite personal appearance was with YTV's hostess P.J. Jen.

They had one practice together and one pre-game skate. Jeff knew the practice was less than stellar. Players were getting used to their new teammates and there was a lot of pressure. Jeff admits he cringed after the practice but everything clicked when the game started.

When game time came, Jeff ignored the pressure and focused on his game. He was paired up with Harold Druken and Ty Jones. In the first two shifts Jeff scored two goals. He had a breakaway goal that knocked the water bottle off the net. The crowd of fifteen thousand at Maple Leaf

Jeff Zehr, No. 55 – Top Prospects Challenge, February 1997
Photograph courtesy of the CHL and Dan Hamilton, Vantage Point Studios

Gardens went wild. It was an incredible moment for the young player—definitely one for the scrapbook. Any residual nervousness was blown away and Jeff enjoyed the rest of the game. His team logged a seven-two victory over Team Cherry.

Randy Copley, Cape Breton Screaming Eagles, 1998

Randy received his invitation to the 1998 Prospects game at the same time he learned he was going to the QMJHL All-Star game. Since the All-Star game was first, Randy was more concerned about that game. Once it was over he started counting the days until he would be heading to Maple Leaf Gardens.

Randy and Moosehead's Alex Tanguay arrived early. They got to catch an OHL game at St. Mike's Arena. Randy admits that he wasn't paying much attention to the game. He was sitting with Bobby Orr at the time, so who could blame him?

The teams had a practice and the skills competition on Monday. It was a pretty full day. The practices were very high tempo and drew a crowd. The players vied in competitions for sprints, skating, puck handling and hardest shot.

Randy Copley, No. 32
Top Prospects Challenge, February 1998
Photograph courtesy of the CHL and Dan Hamilton, Vantage Point Studios

Part of Team Orr, Randy was paired up with number-one-rated prospect Vincent LeCavalier and Simon Gagne for the big game. When it was time to play Randy tried to stick to his style. He is a winger who plays both ends, goes in the corners and does his job. It was a high-profile crowd but Randy just kept his mind on the game.

The quality of the game was outstanding. "Everyone would read the play, players really played their positions and the reaction time was excellent." Even without a lot of time to adjust to new linemates, the teams clicked well.

Although they lost out to Team Cherry, Randy still cited it as a memorable experience and values the chance to be part of it.

Randy must have made a good impression because he was selected in the June NHL Entry Draft by the New York Rangers.

NHL TRAINING CAMPS

The CHL recognizes that young players are anxious to make it to the next level. The league helps players by having a flexible arrangement with the NHL. The CHL allows young players to stay with their NHL teams without losing their CHL eligibility. This distinguishes the league from the NCAA leagues. This means that players can stay with their NHL teams and maybe play a few exhibition games before being sent down to junior.

Going to camp is a big step for young players. Being drafted just opens the door. If you want to come inside, you have to earn it. Even high draft choices can come away without a contract or a spot on the team. Camp can be a real eye opener for young players as they get a taste of the level of play in the NHL.

Getting to stay is a hard-won honour and players need to make a big impression at camp. This can be tough when the guy with the locker next to you has a Stanley Cup ring and his face was on your cereal box when you grew up. It is a big step when training camps roll around and young players prepare to hit NHL ice with NHL players.

Coach Tom Watt shares his advice on how to prepare for camp and make a good impression.

A Coach's Perspective: *Tom Watt, Sudbury Wolves*

If you are going to make a good impression it helps to know what to expect. Coach Tom Watt is just the person to provide that advice. Watt is currently coaching the OHL Sudbury Wolves but he has logged a lot of time in the NHL. He coached the Winnipeg Jets (1981-84), Vancouver Canucks (1985-87) and Toronto Maple Leafs (1990-92).

It was not something he had planned on when he was growing up. With only six teams in the NHL, coaching one didn't seem like a realistic goal. Watt's coaching talents found another venue. He spent fifteen years at the University of Toronto before leaving to coach Canada's 1980 Olympic team under General Manager Father Dave Bauer. From there he went on to coach in Winnipeg.

Watt then became involved in scouting and player development with the Toronto Maple Leafs. He missed being behind the bench and decided to get back to coaching. When a position came up at the beginning of the 1997 season he joined the coaching staff of the Sudbury Wolves.

During his time in the NHL, Watt saw a lot of young players coming to camps. When most players come to camp, you get a look for about a week and send them back down. Some clubs have a rookie camp but most integrate the young players with the veterans. The GMs and scouts want to see how these prospects pan out against NHLers. Some players do manage to hang on a bit longer. One of Watt's players, Paul Mara (Sudbury Wolves), missed the start of the season because the eighteen-year-old stayed with his NHL team. As a Major Junior player he had that flexibility.

Big things are expected of high draft choices. Great expectations can actually be trouble for young prospects. They are often expected to step up quickly and save floundering teams. Watt cites Cam Neely as a young player who played well as a nineteen-to-twenty-year-old but the team needed its top choice to be great and traded him to Boston. In Boston, Neely matured into that great player. The pressure can be tough for a kid.

Watt recognizes there are some players who step up right away. One young rookie who played for Watt when he coached in Winnipeg was Dale Hawerchuk. He stepped into the league as an eighteen-year-old and won the Calder Trophy. Hawerchuk is the exception, not the rule. Watt cites the league's tendency to overlook late bloomers as one of its biggest failings. He points out there can be huge differences between an eighteen-year-old and a twenty-two-year-old and it is important not to discount a player too quickly.

So what happens when the week is up and it is time to go back down? Watt has seen players come away from an NHL camp with new determination. They have had a taste and know what it takes. They want to go back next year and make the team. Getting a taste also helps players to get over the natural intimidation they feel playing with the guy in the scrapbook. Players can be in awe but they still have to perform. Watt notes that players are often more ready to play at the second camp.

Watt offers two pieces of advice to young players who will attend NHL camps.

Get In Shape: Not OK Shape, Game Shape.

Watt notes that many young players aren't as diligent in training as they should be. In the Major Junior league, skill takes them to the top. In the NHL everyone is talented and they are bigger, stronger guys. Players need superior strength and endurance to play at this level.

As a former director of player development, Watt knows that NHL teams have a huge investment in young players. They provide players with training programs for the summer designed to help them get in shape. There will be rigorous physical testing at the camp; players are told what to expect and in return they are expected to come prepared. The results of the testing are discussed with the player. The NHL club's monitoring of the player doesn't end when the week is up. The club will continue to keep a close eye on its prospects.

Watt acknowledges that between the hockey schedule and school, young players do not have a lot of time to train during the season. Players have to look for the gaps in the schedule and have the discipline and desire to keep training.

The commitment doesn't end with the hockey season. The off-season is not a break, it is the time when players need to work on developing cardio endurance, muscular strength and flexibility; the things they may not have had time to do during the season. Players return home for the summer and are out from under the watchful eye of their teams. They need self-discipline to train in the summer.

If you are thinking that you should take the summer off and just work out—think again. Watt thinks players should get jobs in the summer. You cannot spend every minute in the gym, so players who are supposedly taking the summer off to train tend to slack off. Watt recommends getting a physically demanding job. Which is tougher, eight hours of manual labour or a few hours at the gym? Time management is important and players who are used to balancing multiple responsibilities are better able to timetable themselves when the schedule gets hectic.

Learn to Play Without the Puck

Watt's second piece of advice to young players may seem like a strange suggestion—it's not. The reality is that it is a lot harder to get the puck in the NHL. Result—young players spend more time without it. Players may have been drafted for their strong offensive stats but they need to learn to play defensively. This can be a difficult adjustment for young players who are accustomed to dominating the game. They now find themselves continually chasing the puck. Watt's advice—get used to it and get good at it.

Packed and Ready to Play: Players' Experiences At Camp

Derrick Walser, Rimouski Oceanic

Derrick Walser was a player who despite an impressive season was overlooked in the Entry Draft. When the dust had settled he got a phone call. The call was an invite from Coach Alain Vigneault to attend The Montreal Canadien's training camp in August. Since Vigneault had coached in the QMJHL he knew what Walser had to offer and wanted to get a look at him in camp. Walser was pleased and impressed that Vigneault had called personally.

Walser knew that players do make it to the NHL without being drafted and he intended to be one of them. That meant he needed to make a solid impression at camp. Vigneault and Assistant Coach Clement Jodoin were both familiar with Walser's play from Major Junior. Walser made it his mission at camp to make a positive impression on Assistant Coach Dave King.

When it came to preparing for camp Derrick called a friend who had attended pro camps to get some insight into what to expect. He explained about the physical testing Derrick could expect when he got to camp and gave him some tips on what it would be like. The team also sent along a program to help ensure that he would be in shape for camp. Walser found the program similar to what he already did but spent some extra time on weaker areas.

Players are paired up and assigned to a hotel room when they get to camp. There is no one to get you up and moving in the morning. Players are given their schedules and expected to show up.

Initial reaction to the camp: "You are like a shy little kid; it's like going to school for the first time." Walser notes that when you first get on the ice you are nervous and then you start to loosen up. It is weird being on the ice with players like Saku Koivu and Shane Corson. You don't want to hit anybody; they are stars and deserve respect. This is your chance to make an impression and you have to play really hard. The game is faster and the players are stronger. It is a big step up from Major Junior.

Walser was one of the early cuts at camp but he came away with a good feeling. During his time in camp he sat down with Dave King and reviewed his strong points and weak points. Walser knows what he has to work on to improve and has a renewed determination to come back better and stronger next year.

Jeff Zehr, Erie Otters

When Jeff Zehr headed to the New York Islanders camp he already knew the players. The day after the draft the Islanders arranged for their top three picks to attend a conditioning camp. Zehr had hoped to draft well but had no idea that the New York Islanders would make the Otters' left wing their third choice in the 1997 draft.

Fortunately Jeff was in good shape when he went to the conditioning camp. There was physical testing at the NHL draft. Jeff thinks that the physical testing is becoming an important part of the selection process.

The three prospects got to meet the rest of the team at the camp. Jeff admits this early introduction made the August camp easier. His first night in New York he went on a boat cruise with Todd Bertuzzi and Bryan Berard, both OHL graduates. The players were welcoming and tried to make the young prospects comfortable.

When it came time for camp Jeff's initial impression was speed. Everything was so fast, you really had to be quick to keep up. Other skills you had to acquire quickly were timing and positioning. You had to keep yourself in the play.

Jeff was also getting some lessons in work ethic from Coach Rick Bowness. He was pleased with the interest and hoped it was a sign that the team was giving him serious consideration. During the camp he got to play with Islanders star Ziggy Palffy. He was paired with LaPointe and Vukota during the team's exhibition game against the Carolina Hurricanes.

Advice for rookies—you just have to play your game. Checkers check, scorers score. You just go out and do what the team drafted you for. During the camp you have to go hard and stay really focused.

Don MacLean, Hull Olympiques

Halifax native Don MacLean headed south for his first pro camp. A second-round draft pick by the Los Angeles Kings in 1995, Don trained hard during the summer to prepare for the camp. The team sent him a program after he was drafted and he tried to follow it.

The first year Don admits you are pretty intimidated. The players are people you watched as a kid and all of a sudden you are sitting right next to them. Players like Rob Blake and Wayne Gretzky are big names and you get kind of scared. Don remembers being at a team barbecue and Wayne Gretzky and wife Janet sitting down next to him. Gretzky was friendly but Don was too much in awe to really talk to him.

Don stayed at camp for a week his first year before returning to his junior team. The second year he was a little more relaxed. He stayed up with the team to play an exhibition game. He also signed a contract before returning to his junior team.

His junior season was a big one. The Hull Olympiques won the Memorial Cup. Don feels that win was important. He was able to show the Kings what he could do and it was a big confidence builder.

When Don went to camp the third time he was more comfortable and more focused. He was confident and ready to play. This time he was there to earn a spot and he felt that he really had an opportunity.

When you are at camp you are fighting for a job. You have to do your best every time you are on the ice. If you want to stay, you work hard every shift and every practice. It is also important to learn. You learn from the other players, from the coach and from the trainers. Even if you are a top junior player there is still so much more to learn and you have to be willing to listen.

When training camp ended Don stayed. He stayed through the exhibition games and he stayed through the start of the regular season. Don admits there are times when he could not believe that he was really there but once you get on the ice you have to play like a professional.

Now that he has played in the league Don has had a better chance to assess NHL hockey. His assessment: it is amazing. Everyone is good. The game is faster, the passes are on all the time, players play their positions.

Don admits that the pay is good in the NHL but you still get the brutal road trips. The team flies but zipping through time zones is tough even if it is only a two-hour flight. During his first month on the team Don spent two weeks on the road. The CHL is good practice for the lifestyle in the NHL.

His first NHL goal was a very exciting moment for Don. He may have been over the "NHL awe factor" but actually scoring in the NHL was still very special. One disappointment for Don was Mario LeMieux's retirement. He would have liked to play against the Magnificent One.

Despite being only twenty and coming right out of Major Junior, Don managed to stay with the team until after Christmas. He was then sent down to the team's minor league affiliate, the Fredericton Canadiens. Don is not bitter about being sent down. He had not dressed for ten games prior to being sent down so he had some warning.

As a member of the Kings' AHL team, Don is focused on playing hard, learning and getting back up to the NHL as soon as possible. He now knows what it takes to play in that league and he knows he can play at that level.

Chapter 14

IN THE STANDS: SCOUTS ON SCOUTING

THE PROMISE OF EXPOSURE raises the question of whom players are performing for. The answer is the scouts. These are the guys who will analyze the player's performance and make recommendations on whether he will get drafted. Do you like to watch a lot of hockey? Want to be the one to discover new talent? That's part of what scouts do but it is not an easy job. The industry is competitive, the investment enormous and the travel schedule hectic; but the guys who do the job love it.

There are many different kinds of scouts. NHL teams and CHL teams scout draft-eligible and veteran players. Some scouts work full time and others free-lance, working within a small region. Talent is spread out and teams need to have scouts checking out the talent everywhere from rural Canada to Russia.

Hockey is spreading and there is a demand for players for non-NHL teams. Organizations like PowerPlay International hire scouts to secure likely prospects for European and American Pro Minor leagues. Three scouts took some time from the rink to explain the job. All three scouts work for different organizations and have different criteria when it comes to selecting players.

Dan Marr is the former Scouting Coordinator for the Toronto Maple Leafs. He was focused on preparing a list for the NHL Entry Draft.

Barry Trapp is currently the Director of Scouting for the national program. It is his job to scout the players who will represent Canada in international tournaments. He is also a ten-year veteran of the Central Scouting Bureau (CSB), an independent organization that ranks young NHL prospects.

Harry Boyd is a scouting consultant for an independent organization that helps minor professional teams in North America and Europe find players for their rosters. He also has logged twenty-three years as a regional scout for the New York Islanders.

SCOUTING FOR THE LEAFS: DAN MARR, SCOUTING COORDINATOR

Since you can't take Scouting 101 at the local college you may wonder how Dan Marr managed to end up in his current job. He started out playing hockey and by his own admission, "wasn't exactly the best player."

What he ended up becoming was an athletic therapist. He graduated from Sheridan College in 1980 and went to work with the Toronto Marlboroughs. He spent a year in Newmarket with the Leafs' farm team before moving on to work with the Toronto Maple Leafs as an athletic therapist.

Marr would often talk about players with Leafs executives Gord Stellick and Floyd Smith. Evidently he had a good read on players because he was asked to join the scouting staff. At first Marr said no; after all he was trained as an athletic therapist, not a scout. However, he reconsidered and decided that he was ready for a career change. Scouting would let him explore a different aspect of the game.

His first year in scouting he was responsible for the west. That meant all the junior and college players. The western stint was short-lived and by Christmas Marr was back in Ontario, this time in Windsor. Eventually he was able to relocate back to Toronto, and that was his home base. Marr made another career move and started the 1998-99 season as the head scout for the new Atlanta Thrashers.

Doing The Job

Every fan is a couch scout but when you put your professional reputation on the line with your decisions, you take a little extra time. Marr really evaluates the way he arrives at a decision; sometimes you see a player and scout with your heart, not with your brain. A professional scout cannot afford to make decisions that way. You have to carefully and critically assess a player to determine if he will be a prospect.

Scouts do not always select the same players. Every scout has his own criteria for a prospect. However, your checklist aside, when you run into a really good skilled player you sit up and take notice. Younger players are not fully developed. You have to make a judgment call as to whether they will "fill out" as players. As an example Marr cited Eric Daze, a Chicago fourth-round draft pick. He was not a strong skater but he had great hands.

Marr spends between five and six months on the road every year. An NHL scout will often see as many as thirty games in a month. That's a lot of hockey even for a serious fan. Marr does not have a particular region. He is a rover who double checks all the regions to provide a comparative assessment of the talent. The Leafs have scouts in all the regions in North America and Marr coordinates their activities.

When Marr travels he has lists and reports on the prospects identified by the regional scout. Marr always keeps his eyes open; no one wants to overlook a potential superstar. His main focus is providing an assessment of the higher-ranked prospects.

Looking Around

So where are the scouts looking these days? Everywhere. Marr admits that the CHL is a major source of young talent and historically some of the best players come out of this system. He notes that junior players tend to be developed more quickly. These players are brought up into a pro program. The junior system is like a prep school for the NHL.

That doesn't mean other sources of players are ignored. Scouts are looking south of the border. Marr notes that the U.S. hockey program has become much stronger as proven by the steady stream of young players coming through that system. The Leafs scouts also cover Europe on a regular basis. With Captain Mats Sundin front and centre for the team there is no doubt about the potential of European players.

Some events that see a lot of scouts in the stands are the World Junior Tournament and the CHL Prospects game. These events feature top young players and allow scouts to see the players against their peers. It is sometimes difficult if a team is weak or strong to assess a particular player. By seeing the players in another context a scout can get a different perspective on a prospect.

Testing the Talent

Physical testing is a big part of determining the potential of young players. Scouts look very seriously at the results. Marr credits the Major Junior teams with doing a good job of preparing their players. The teams do testing so players will know what to expect and they also promote proper training and conditioning.

Another source of conditioning information for the young players is the agents. Most agents enroll their clients in summer programs or help choose a personal trainer. Education about proper nutrition and training is very important for the players whatever the source as long as the players are getting proper information.

When it comes to doing the testing the Leafs have a bit of a break. The organization that does the testing for NHL, the Central Scouting Bureau, is the same organization the Leafs use so they can rely on Central Scouting's fitness assessment of the players. Marr admits that occasionally they do bring in players for testing.

Making the Assessment

Marr admits every scout has his own formula, certain qualities he wants to identify in a player. Some of the common criteria are size, skating, puck handling skills, and hockey sense. Another less measurable factor is character. Scouts are not the only people hanging around the rink. They will often talk to agents and coaches. Admittedly those opinions can be less than objective but you can get some valuable information.

A good way to get a sense of the player is to talk to opposing coaches. They don't see the player every day but they play against him enough to get a sense of him on the ice. Scouts can get an idea about character from the player's activities in the community and performance at school.

Since Marr is concerned with draft-eligible players these players may be in their rookie seasons and that can translate into not much ice time. Marr notes that the junior teams do a very good job of scouting and if the players went high in the Major Junior Draft you give those players a careful look. Scouts will also attend practices to get another look.

With so many players available, keeping careful records is an important part of a scout's job. Marr uses a computer system to keep track of players' reports. He also uses a manual system that allows him to shuffle players around during the season.

Meeting the Players

Players know (or hope) they are being scouted during their draft year. In addition to seeing them in the stands, players often speak to scouts during their draft year. The Leafs try to speak to prospects on Major Junior teams prior to Christmas. These interviews don't come as a surprise to the prospects and most are prepared by their agents.

Marr likes to interview the players early before their answers get too pat. He does recognize that players can be nervous about their interviews and they may come off a bit stiff. The Leafs stop interviewing players in

146

February. The players are gearing up for the playoffs and Marr wants to let them focus on hockey.

A Scout's Opinion

Scouts get input from General Managers in developing a draft strategy based on the needs of the team. Most General Managers do listen to the scouts. The scouts are the ones who see the players night after night and General Managers let them do their job. The main focus for Marr is amateur scouting, and that means Marr's primary responsibility is putting a list together for the annual Entry Draft.

Getting the List Ready

The Scouts start putting together the regional lists and in January they have a meeting. As the season progresses the team has a good idea where it will be drafting and the scouting becomes more intense. Marr increases the level of crossover scouting as he tries to isolate its group of prospects for the draft.

Scouts eventually put together a list for the draft. There is a lot of back-and-forth between the scouting staff before a rough draft of the list is prepared. The team likes to follow the list as closely as possible during the draft. Certain players generate a lot of excitement every year. They are projected to go in the first round and usually do. Scouting involves more than just knowing the top prospects. It means knowing who is likely to be available at every level of the draft.

Teams keep their preferences confidential. Despite the advance interviews most players do not know which teams are likely to draft them. It is a very competitive industry so teams keep quiet about their views on prospects.

The team has its "first round" of players and is sometimes lucky enough to get one of those players, maybe in the third round. Occasionally you catch a break and a player you see as high potential is still available later in the draft. Different teams are looking for different criteria in players.

In Final Analysis

Scouts are not always right. Choosing young players who will develop into NHL talent is a tough call. Some prospects do not realize their potential and every year undrafted players come to camp and make an impression. Doing a good job means being right more often than you are wrong. Marr's work ends when the players are drafted but he does keep an eye on the players coming up. You always want to know if you were right and if the potential that made you favour a player is realized.

SCOUTING FOR CANADA: BARRY TRAPP, DIRECTOR OF SCOUTING

Like most Canadians, Barry Trapp began his career in hockey as a player. When his playing days were over Trapp took up a spot behind the bench. Trapp coached Midget and Tier II in Saskatchewan. He went on to coach in the WHL, first for Regina and then for Moose Jaw.

Getting the Job

After coaching, Trapp decided to try out another hockey position, taking a job at the Central Scouting Bureau. Trapp spent ten years with CSB, five of those years as Chief Scout.

With such an impressive hockey resume you can see why Trapp is the Director of Scouting for Canadian Hockey. The question is what made him leave the CSB? Trapp was at the World Junior Cup Tournament in Boston in 1995. The gold-winning team impressed him so much he decided if he ever got the opportunity to work for his country he would take it.

The opportunity came quickly. When Trapp was attending the NHL Draft in St. Louis he ran into the incumbent Director of Scouting for Canada Hockey, Ray Payne. Payne was leaving the program to go to San Jose. Trapp sent off a resume and waited. After two weeks he decided they were not interested and prepared to go back to CSB. He was wrong; he got the call from Canada Hockey Vice President Bob Nicholson. The national program had found its new Director of Scouting.

Working For Canada Hockey

Trapp has been with the program several seasons. He is part of the Canada Hockey team and that is a feeling he enjoys. The Central Scouting Bureau is an independent ranking system and doesn't give you the sense of working for a team. Trapp loves having the opportunity to work with Canada Hockey.

His job involves more than picking the young Canadians for the WJC and the Under-18 Tournament. The national hockey program involves any Canadian, man or woman, who puts on a Canadian jersey. Trapp admits that with Canada fielding an Olympic team including NHLers, the responsibility for selecting that team is mainly with the GM of the Olympic team.

Travel Time

Trapp's job is never really done. After every international tournament there is always next year's team to scout. When Trapp gets back from the World Junior Cup he usually takes about a week off before getting back to scouting. With fifty-four CHL teams in Canada and talented young Canadians playing in the American university system, Trapp does a lot of traveling.

He is also responsible for scouting the competition and that means heading overseas. He attends European tournaments to get a look at the players Team Canada might face. It does get difficult being away from home so much but Trapp loves working with the national program.

The initial list for the WJC has to be prepared for the August evaluation camp. While forty-two players are invited in August, only thirty-two are invited to the December camp. Sometimes players are added or deleted from the list. When the CHL season starts, so do Trapp's road trips.

This native of Fort Qu'Appelle, Saskatchewan starts his circuit in the WHL before moving east to the OHL and QMJHL. After an initial look Trapp will crisscross the country checking and re-checking players. When it comes to selecting players, Trapp is adamant that there is no quota system. He is looking for the best players for the team, not a politically correct blend of players. There is also no quota when it comes to age.

Making an Assessment

The job involves a careful assessment of players. Trapp does have some priorities when assessing players but keeps an eye out for players who are really stepping up. With an Under-18 team to field, Trapp is always checking players for current and future teams.

With so many teams and so little time Trapp gets some help from technology. The internet gives Trapp the statistics for the teams. Since the Canada Hockey scouting staff is just Trapp he is not above getting some assistance from other scouts. As a former Director of the CSB, Trapp can usually count on some insight from the organization.

As a veteran scout, Trapp has friends in the fraternity who will offer a second opinion if Trapp feels he needs another take on a player. The assistance does not translate to pressure when it comes to selecting players.

Making Cuts

Trapp admits making cuts is tough. Playing for their country means a lot to young players and it can be heartbreaking when the last cuts are made. It is tough to put together a team when there are so many talented players. You have to focus on getting the correct blend and sometimes that means filling certain roles.

SCOUTING FOR POWERPLAY INTERNATIONAL: HARRY BOYD

This twenty-three-year veteran of scouting has occupied just about every hockey job available. Boyd is a former University of Toronto player and spent some time playing hockey in Italy. Back in the 1940s hockey wasn't much of a career choice. There were only six NHL teams and the pay was not great. In non-hockey work Boyd was a high school teacher. He was also the school's coach and took the team to the Provincial Championships.

Boyd eventually became a coach in the Ontario Minor Hockey system. Boyd started coaching Peewee for the most common reason: his son was playing. The team performed well and won the Ontario championships and went to Quebec for a tournament. The presence of future NHLer Steve Shutt was probably a big help to the young team. Boyd coached his way through the system from Bantam to Junior "B."

Canada is not the only country to benefit from Boyd's coaching expertise. He took a sabbatical and headed overseas to coach in Vienna's professional league. Boyd was not the only Canadian. Canadians were exploring the opportunities to be had in international hockey.

Scouting for the New York Islanders

When Boyd returned from his European stint the New York Islanders were looking for a regional scout. Boyd got a call from management to see if he was interested. He was. In 1974 Boyd hung up his whistle and got out his notebook.

With so many leagues and teams, professional teams often employ regional scouts to ensure that they do not miss any hot prospects. Boyd's territory was mainly teams within driving distance of Toronto. He would occasionally take a road trip when the Islanders wanted a second opinion on a particular prospect.

In addition to scouting for the Islanders, Boyd had some other interests. He acted as a scout for the OHL's Kingston Canadians and was the Assistant Head Scout for the OHL. Boyd's activities were not confined to scouting. He is also the former owner of a Tier II Club, the North York Rangers.

When it comes to scouting Boyd admits it is a hidden job market. You tend to meet people in the industry and opportunities arise informally. He spent twenty-three years as a regional scout for the New York Islanders.

The Other Pro Leagues

At seventy most Canadians are enjoying retirement but Boyd is still active as a scout. Currently, he is working for a Philadelphia-based company called PowerPlay International. The company provides assistance to minor professional teams in the United States and Europe in finding players. For players who are overlooked by the NHL and want to extend their careers there are numerous opportunities in these leagues.

Boyd focuses on Major Junior players who are ending their careers and players in Canadian universities. This is a particularly good option for smaller players who are being overlooked by the NHL. European teams are less concerned with size. Boyd notes that players can do very well financially in countries like Germany.

Boyd has had experience as both a player and a coach in Europe and has really seen hockey explode as an international sport. He remembers playing the Chinese National Team when he was in Vienna. At the time the team was more interested in the making of artificial ice but it was a sign of hockey's spreading popularity. With Canada's long history in the sport, Canadians are much in demand in other countries as coaches and players.

Some players have moved on with non-hockey careers but other older players are interested in getting in a couple more years of competitive hockey. Players who make the list are often invited to training camps. Boyd knows one player who is now with a minor pro team in Hampton and another player who is in Europe.

Young Talent

With selections being made so early, Boyd notes that late bloomers can be overlooked. He cited Mighty Ducks centre Paul Kariya as a player who might have been overlooked at eighteen because he was a smaller player but in his twenties he exhibits remarkable talent. An unfortunate effect of early selection is that players might lose confidence and motivation if they cannot make a quick step into the NHL. These late bloomers can be successful in other leagues.

Chapter 15

LIFESTYLES OF THE YOUNG AND TALENTED

The life of a Major Junior hockey player isn't all fun and games. OK, maybe it is almost all games. You play hockey all the time, you get scouted by NHL scouts, you get to travel . . . it sounds glamorous. What it really is, is hard work.

The practices, the games, the grueling road trips and school add up to a very long season. It is a lifestyle that promotes effective time management. There is more to adjusting to the league than learning about hockey. Players make big moves and that means big lifestyle changes.

MOVING AWAY FROM HOME

Every year players pack up and head for their CHL cities. Where do these relocated young athletes live? Most teams make arrangements for the players to live with billet families, carefully chosen to provide a home for the player during the season. Teams favour the family atmosphere and supportive environment provided by a family.

New Homes: A Team's Perspective

When players move away to pursue their hockey dreams they are moving to new teams, new cities and new homes. Those homes are carefully chosen by the teams. Dave Harris is the Manager of Operations for the new Mississauga Ice Dogs. Dave had to find homes for the players who would be joining this new franchise. The Dogs use the term "land-parents," a term that reflects the landlord/surrogate parent responsibilities. Other common terms include "billets," "hockey families" and "pensions." What it means to players is home for the season.

For the Ice Dog debut in the 1998-99 season, the search for families began in February 1998. Ads were placed in local papers asking for volunteers. The team likes to keep players in a relatively small geographical area, close to the rink and to school. The volunteers were invited to an information session where they were told about their role and responsibilities for the young players. Dave stressed that being a land-parent is not a money-making proposition. The three hundred-and-fifty dollars per month paid to the families will barely cover groceries for a young athlete. The Peel Regional Police are also present at the information session to explain the background checks that prospective land-parents will face.

If families decide to go ahead despite the nominal income and security check, they will be interviewed by the team and a representative will visit the family. Harris indicates that they do not really have specific criteria; each family is assessed individually. The player is expected to have his own room or if he shares a room it is with another team member.

Information about the family and the home is gathered by the team. They look at the size and location of the home, the player's room, the number of children, the presence of pets, and things like whether the home has smokers.

In addition to gathering information about the families, the team gathers information from the players. Players fill out a form providing information about their families, siblings, pets, religion. The teams use the information to match players with compatible families.

If a family takes a player it has a responsibility to act as a surrogate family. The players are also expected to help out around the house and obey house rules. One area where the team does step in is transportation. Because of the hectic schedules, the team makes sure that players have rides to and from practices, games and team events.

Sometimes a player and his land-parents are not a good fit. If problems arise the team likes to try to talk things out with the player and family. Sometimes players are moved. One Ice Dog player was living with a family with a Newfoundland dog—the player was not a pet person and that type of dog is a very big pet. The player remains in contact with the family but has chosen to live in another household. The family will be still be considered for new (and dog-loving) players.

The team wants the player in a comfortable home environment and it tries to support bonding opportunities for the new family units. The team has a section in the rink reserved for the player's hockey family; and the land-parents are invited to team functions like Christmas parties and special event dinners.

Players' Perspectives On Moving Away From Home

Stephen Peat, Red Deer Rebels

When Stephen made the trip from Langley, B.C. he knew he would be joining the Red Deer Rebels but not where he would be living. He was picked up at the airport and taken to his new home. Some players were doubled up but the only player that Peat shares the house with is the three-year-old son of his billet family. So far his game is banging his stick on the floor but he makes up in enthusiasm what he lacks in skill.

Stephen Peat, No. 10
Top Prospects Challenge,
February 1998
Photograph courtesy of the CHL and Dan Hamilton, Vantage Point Studios

The laundry and cooking are done for Stephen but he is expected to clean his room and pick up his stuff. Stephen admits that when it comes to chores it was tougher at home. The billet family basically follows the team's rules when it comes to curfews. He does miss his parents and younger brother. His brother is playing B.C. Junior hockey.

Stephen's initial shyness kept him out from under foot during his early days with the family. He tried to be out of the house or in his room. His billet family was understanding. They gave Stephen his space and enough time to get used to living in a new place. And it does take some adjustment. It is hard living with a family that you don't really know. Stephen sees Christmas of the rookie season as the high water mark. The players get home for a brief visit during the holidays, usually five or six days, and the team picks up the tab for the trip.

Christmas is not the only time that Stephen gets to see his parents. His mom tries to visit him in Red Deer every couple of months and the Peats will try to see their son when road trips bring him closer to home. The team tries to give players some time after a game to visit with parents.

155

Stephen has gotten to know his billet family. He stayed with them for the second year. Former players do keep in touch and he will do the same when he leaves Red Deer.

Larry Paleczny, Owen Sound Platers

When Larry first arrived in Belleville he went right to the rink. The players were told who their billets would be and taken to their new homes. Players are usually told a bit about what their billet families do and how long they have been billeting players. In some cases the family will take two players. It is fairly common for players to be doubled up; it gives them someone to hang out with.

Sometimes a billet family and a player do not click. That happened in Larry's first year. The team wants players to be comfortable and will move them if they are not happy with their living arrangements. Larry was very happy in his second billet home until a trade early in his second season moved him to Owen Sound. In the new city, he was doubled up with another player. He got along well with his housemate and it helped him settle in after the mid-season move.

Both in Belleville and in Owen Sound the team rather than the family makes the rules. The biggest rule relates to curfew. Being old enough to vote doesn't mean Larry can ignore curfew. The team will call players in random checks to ensure they are home on time.

Despite being nineteen Larry is still billeting. The teams want players to stay in a family environment. They are extremely busy and the families do the shopping and cooking. Originally Larry was doubled up with an older player but now that he is older he is the only player living with his family.

Mathieu Biron, Shawinigan Cataractes

In the Quebec league billeting is called pensioning but the drill is pretty much the same. Young players are paired up with "hockey families" during the season. Although his older brother Martin played in the Quebec league he couldn't really offer much advice about billeting. Martin lived at home when he was playing for Beauport and with family friends when he was traded to Hull.

Mathieu met his pension family when he arrived at camp. He was the family's first player. When he arrived, he was also their only player. A mid-season trade gave Mathieu a housemate.

The only rule in the house is that player and family respect each other. The team imposes an 11:00 p.m. curfew, which is always in effect unless the players are told otherwise by the coach.

Mathieu is responsible for keeping his room clean. He will occasionally help out with chores but with his hectic schedule he rarely has time. The family provides meals and usually checks to see what Mathieu likes. He is pretty flexible except for pre-game meals. He is very careful about what he eats before a game, usually choosing pasta.

Mathieu admits he is luckier than most players. His parents live about an hour and a half away, and the Birons are at most of Mathieu's games and call almost every day. The drive to Shawinigan is not the only hockey road trip the Birons take. They also make the trek down to Rochester, New York to catch his brother Martin's games.

It is tougher for guys who are farther away from home. It is not just leaving your family, you also leave your friends (and sometimes your girlfriend) as well. Before Christmas, Mathieu got two weekends off and was able to travel home and catch up with his friends.

Players do make new friends when they join the team. Most of Mathieu's friends are teammates. This is convenient, since he spends most of his time at the rink or on the bus. He does have some friends at his new school but does not get to see them very often outside of school.

Things have worked out well for Mathieu. He has developed a good relationship with his pension family and is adjusting to sharing digs with another player. Mathieu considers himself a pretty independent guy and likes the responsibility of being on his own.

LIFE IN THE LEAGUE: PLAYERS' PERSPECTIVES

Alex Johnstone, Halifax Mooseheads

Halifax Moosehead Alex Johnstone keeps busy during the season, on ice and off. One

Mathieu Biron, No. 34
1998 Top Prospects Challenge
Photograph courtesy of the CHL and Dan Hamilton, Vantage Point Studios

year he carried a full courseload and it was difficult. The following year he took only two courses, as his school obligations lightened up. He had some help from a tutor arranged and paid for by the Mooseheads. When you miss a week of school it helps to have someone to catch up with.

Alex may have had fewer courses but this doesn't mean he had more time to lounge around. The Mooseheads are very active in the community. Alex's favourite activity was visiting the young patients at Halifax's I.W.K. Children's Hospital. The kids were enthusiastic fans and loved to see the players. Players also regularly visited local junior high school students.

Alex recently did a radio commercial for the Red Cross. The commercial was a caution about safety and natural ice. The team is careful to arrange the players' community activities around the school schedule.

Community involvement can lead to new skills. Alex and former team captain Jody Shelley learned how to play ringette when they gave

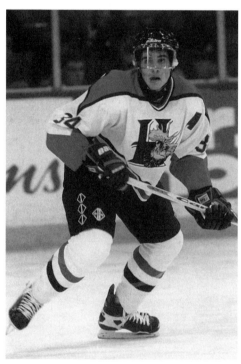

some skating tips to a Junior High ringette team. He worked on his golf game. He and other Mooseheads were frequent participants in summer tournaments. It was a busy life but Alex enjoyed it. He met a lot of people in the community. The busy schedule helped him develop time management and planning skills but he did appreciate the occasional day off.

Alex also spent a lot of time with the police and no, he is not on parole. Since entering the league in 1994 the Mooseheads have a program that matches the players to local police officers. All the officers volunteer to act as "big brothers" to the players. Alex often played pool,

Alex Johnstone, No. 34
Halifax Mooseheads
Photograph courtesy of Terry Waterfield

158

grabbed a bite or hit the firing range with his police officer. If you ever need the police in Halifax the rink is a good place to look. It is not unusual to see half a dozen off-duty officers hanging out to watch the games.

Being a draft-eligible player Alex focused on ending the season in excellent shape. He tried to squeeze in workouts and sometimes it was a very tight squeeze. The team has practice every day at 4:30 p.m. unless it is a game day. On game days the team has a 10:00 a.m. practice that is usually light.

After school, community activities, the gym, and practice, Alex headed home for dinner and did some homework before turning in. During his rookie year Alex wondered if he would be able to manage. It was a long season for the young player and he was tired. Fortunately he adjusted to the pace and play in the league and enjoyed his second season.

Being tired provides one advantage for a player; you don't mind an early curfew. The night before a game Alex would be home at ten o'clock. This was tough when it was Friday night and all his friends were going out. Alex played in his home town so he had lots of friends outside the sport who didn't have a curfew. Even if there is no game, players have to be home by 11:00 p.m. except for rare nights when the team suspends curfew. Alex recognized that it is part of the commitment that he made to play in an elite league.

The Mooseheads spend a lot of time on the road so in any given week Alex could be anywhere in Quebec. Long bus rides in the middle of the night are not exactly glamorous. When you add rigorous back-to-back games to the trip it is actually a lot of work. A typical two weeks might mean twelve-hour bus rides and eight games in ten nights, home and away.

Patrick DesRochers, Sarnia Sting

Sarnia Sting netminder Patrick DesRochers thinks his life is pretty boring. With a tryout for the national junior team, a spot at the prospects game, and projected to go very high in the 1998 Draft, most young Canadians would find it pretty interesting.

The Sting puts a lot of emphasis on school and Pat gets up in the morning and heads for school. Since most OHL teams are pretty close, Pat does not miss many days. After class Pat heads off to the rink.

The guys get ready for practice and do some light stretching. The team has the ice for two hours but usually spend about an hour and a half on the ice. Some players ride stationary bikes or lift weights. Pat usually rides the bike to get rid of lactic acid buildup in his muscles. As a goaltender he likes to work on his leg strength.

Pat also likes to work on his flexibility. He notes that as you get older you need to work harder to maintain your flexibility. Pat's dad was a goalie and he firmly believed that goalies should be able to do the splits. Since he sent three young goalies to the OHL, maybe that philosophy has merit.

After a shower, Pat heads home to grab some supper. He eats pasta on road trips but is more of a meat-and-potatoes kind of guy. He favours grilled chicken, baked potato and salad as a pre-game meal. If he has homework Pat gets it done after dinner. By the end of the day he is pretty tired and it is usually lights out by ten-thirty.

Like most CHL teams the Sting try to get out to meet their fans. On weekends and in the evening team members often help out with minor league teams. The team also hosts a "Meet the Sting" event for young fans. Pat's favourite event is a charity event that puts the Sting players head-to-head with a local gymnastics team in a fitness contest. He admits the gymnasts are pretty impressive athletes. The players also do radio spots to promote the team and sponsors.

Patrick DesRochers, No. 37
Top Prospects Challenge, February 1998
*Photograph courtesy of the CHL and Dan Hamilton,
Vantage Point Sudios*

As a goalie, Pat gets to let his artistic side show—on his head. He designs the artwork for his helmet. A local artist does the actual painting. Pat started the year with the Stings emblem but has decided on a new look. Pat's helmet now offers an historic look at hockey with classic shots of Bobby Orr, Phil Esposito and Ken Dryden.

In any week during the season there are usually two or three games scheduled. The players are expected to be at the rink by 5:30 p.m. for a 7:30 p.m. game.

The guys will tape sticks and have a team meeting before hitting the ice for a warmup skate. After the game the players have a quick meeting and shower before heading home. Even if Pat is at an away game it is pretty common for his parents to be in the stands. His mom and dad have made the eight-hour drive up to the Soo to catch their youngest son in a game.

When Pat is not in nets he likes to relax by watching movies and hanging out with friends. He recommends getting away from the rink sometimes. It clears your head and keeps you from getting burned out. It can be a long season, especially for a goalie.

Playing nets is a tough job—you are either a hero or a bum. The first goalie selected in the 1998 NHL Entry Draft, Pat is definitely more hero than bum.

Steve Gainey, Kamloops Blazers

Kamloops Blazers winger Steve Gainey learned quickly that playing in the Major Junior league is serious business. It is also a lot of work.

Steve expected Major Junior to be similar to minor hockey. It was not. It is a fast, competitive league.

To help players prepare for games the team has practice every day except a game day. The practice lasts about an hour and a half. Steve likes to do a little extra skating after practice. Some players prefer to ride the bike or lift weights. The team does have an off-ice training program. Steve likes to ride the bike but he keeps the weight lifting light during the season.

Steve sees the rigorous game schedule as a great way to develop as a player. Players step up their play and improve their condi-tioning when they face the

Steve Gainey, No. 16
Kamloops Blazers
Photograph courtesy of the Kamloops Blazers

161

competition in this league. You need to improve to keep up. Like most rookies, Steve did more watching than playing his first season. He had some catching up to do. In his fourth season with the Blazers he saw plenty of ice time.

Like most WHL teams the Blazers spend a lot of time on the road. In a two-week period the team made the drive to play in Spokane, Portland, and Regina. As a veteran Steve has a good spot on the bus. Unlike many players, Steve actually enjoys being on the road. He likens the experience to a traveling slumber party. He watches movies, plays cards and hangs out with teammates. Furthermore, despite the cramped quarters, Steve actually uses his time on the road to catch up on sleep.

Players can put a lot of pressure on themselves; Steve tries to keep relaxed. He focuses on improving his game and developing his conditioning and strength. Despite his best intentions, he is not immune to putting pressure on himself. He scored his first CHL goal late in his rookie season; he was getting worried. His first goal was not a game-winner or particularly spectacular but it was a real relief. Getting that first goal of the season in was not a concern in the 1998-99 season. Steve started out strong with six goals in six games.

The Blazers like to give back to the community. Players who have finished high school meet at the rink on non-game days to get their assignments. Steve is a frequent visitor to local elementary schools, where he often talks to the students about sportsmanship. Players also visit seniors' centres to catch up with their older fans.

When he has a couple of hours off Steve likes to play pool or go to a movie with friends. He has friends on and off the team. It is important to get out of the rink and have other interests. During the summer Steve hits the road for some camping and fishing. He also plays other sports including soccer and golf.

Steve was sad to see the old Montreal Forum replaced. He grew up hoping to one day have the opportunity to play there. Now his sights are set on the new Forum. Steve was a fourth-round pick who improved substantially after his draft year. He signed a contract with his NHL team and it looks like his dream will come true.

MAKING THE JUMP TO JUNIOR: A ROOKIE'S VIEW OF THE LEAGUE

It is a big step up when a player puts on a CHL jersey and hits the ice. It can be tough for a young rookie, far from home and maybe in a little over his head. Every year hundreds of young players make that step and survive, even excel.

Jonathan Cheechoo is a player who made that step with style. The Belleville Bull started his rookie season fourth in scoring and steadily improved his game. In his second season with the team Jonathan shared his experiences of his rookie season in Canada's elite Junior league.

This young player had a long way to travel to pursue his dream. Born in Moose Factory, a small Cree community in Northern Ontario, Jonathan credits his father Merv with helping him develop his playing skills. His dad had been an enthusiastic and skilled player and passed on those traits to Jonathan.

18 month old Jonathan Cheechoo takes to the ice for the first time with father Merv.
Photograph courtesy of the Cheechoo family

The Road To Belleville

Unfortunately, the isolated northern community could not support Jonathan's growing talent and at age fourteen he headed to Timmins, Ontario to play AAA Bantam. Jonathan's family was supportive of his hockey ambitions but he knew they would be equally supportive if he decided to return home. During the early months away from home he was tempted.

The move was tough on the young prospect. He missed his family but loved hockey and had made a commitment to his new team. The first two months were the hardest but Jonathan adjusted and his game continued to develop.

After Timmins, Jon packed up and headed to a AAA Midget team in Kapuskasing. After a stint in this league Jonathan once again packed up, traveling south to Kitchener, Ontario to play Junior "B." His next move came when the Belleville Bulls drafted him fifth overall in the 1997 OHL Draft.

Deciding to Play Major Junior

Always a diligent student, Jonathan caught the attention of NCAA teams. He had a choice to make and he felt that Major Junior offered the best development for a young player. If he went the NCAA route it would mean several years of waiting to play at an elite level. The education package he would get in the OHL would keep his options open if his plans for a career in hockey did not materialize.

Jonathan didn't know much about the league growing up. What he did know was that it would be a higher level of play with an elite group of young players. He also knew that it would be time-consuming. His stint in Kitchener Junior "B" was helpful because he got to know some Kitchener Rangers who answered his questions about the league.

Jonathan prepared questions to ask each of the teams he spoke with prior to the draft. He was careful to check out the education packages of each team. He really wanted to be drafted but he knew he had to be smart about it and that meant being informed about each team.

Jonathan Cheechoo
Moose Factory Minor Hockey
Photograph courtesy of the Cheechoo family

Jonathan's agent, Thane Campbell, a former varsity player and Toronto lawyer, advised him in making these important decisions. They have a very good relationship and speak regularly during the season. Jon admits that it really helps to have someone to go to when you need information or assistance.

The BIG Day

Jonathan was nervous about the OHL Draft. He says, "You never know until they say your name." The teams have their own agendas and a player never really knows if or how he fits into their game plans. Jonathan spoke to a number of teams but they never made any commitments. He "kind of had an idea he would maybe go first round," but he was still really nervous.

Fortunately Jonathan didn't have to wait long to hear his name. Drafting high was nice but Jonathan knew he was still going to have to prove himself. He was not complacent when he went to camp; he went to earn a spot.

Unlike some prospects who are surprised by the teams that step forward to claim them, Jonathan had spoken to Belleville prior to the draft. They had not made any promises but Jon sensed they were interested. He was right.

After the Draft

Jonathan's first taste of Belleville was in July when the team brought its prospects to town for some fitness testing and some "get-to-know-you time." This was a family affair. Jonathan got to meet his future teammates and his parents got to meet the other players' parents.

The next trip down was in August for training camp. The prospects were all housed at a hotel for the three-day camp. The team paid for the first forty-eight hours but in order to preserve their eligibility to play NCAA, players had to pick up the tab for the last day.

Jonathan had been training hard all summer and was ready to go out and earn his spot. The ice surface was bigger and the game was faster but Jonathan stepped up quickly. During the exhibition season Jonathan led the team in scoring, so not surprisingly, he took a place on the Belleville roster.

Being a Rookie

Even with an impressive start to the season, Jonathan was still a rookie in an elite league and he had some learning to do. He was benched for some rookie mistakes; things he had to learn from and improve on. Early in the season he hovered around third in scoring and was a regular second line player for the team, an impressive accomplishment only four months into a rookie season.

I'm Playing Where?

An offensive forward, Jonathan was surprised when he was switched to defence. It was a big adjustment and he was worried. He had been drafted as a forward and he was concerned that he wasn't meeting the expectations of the team. After several games in his new role, he decided to approach the coach.

It was a tough thing for a rookie to do and Jonathan was nervous but he needed to understand his role on the team. His advice to a rookie with questions—ask, but ask in a smart way. An elite team is no place for tantrums or attitude. You have to realise that your coach has reasons for what he is doing.

A conference with the coach revealed those reasons. The team was weak defensively with only one veteran defenceman and Jonathan was a strong skater. He was doing well in the role, but he would not be staying there permanently. This was a big relief and Jonathan got back to playing.

His time as a defenceman had some added benefits. Having always been an aggressively offensive forward, Jonathan was weaker defensively. His stint as a defenceman helped him improve that aspect of his game.

Lots to Learn

Despite years of hockey experience, Jonathan found he still had things to learn. With the bigger ice surface and faster game Jonathan had to pull up his play. There was more to learn than just playing bigger and faster; he also had to learn to play smarter. The coach helped him learn about defensive zone coverage and becoming a better two-way player.

The coach wasn't the only one helping Jonathan's game. The veterans on the team were great about sharing tips with the newcomers. They were also role models. Jonathan says that when you see them go out and play so hard, you want to go out and make the same effort. Playing in this league exposes you to some of the best young talent in hockey and when you play against these guys you learn.

A Traveling League

Major Junior teams log a lot of hours on the bus and Belleville is no exception. Jonathan's AAA Midget team had also been a traveling team so he knew what to expect on the long bus trips. It was the shorter trips that got him. Like most players, Jonathan, when he finally gets to sleep, is a heavy sleeper. Heavy enough to wake up with a ball cap full of shaving cream. These kinds of pranks are common on short trips but don't happen on the longer trips. Players know how tiring long trips can be. Jonathan tries to eat well and rest as much as possible.

A New Home

Once he knew he would be staying with the Bulls, Jonathan was introduced to his new billet family. So were the Cheechoos. To get from Moose Factory to Belleville you have to fly or take a five-hour train ride to the nearest road access and then drive for ten hours. The long trip didn't discourage Jonathan's parents, who were determined to ensure that Jonathan was happily settled in his hockey home.

Several years' experience in billeting made for an easy adjustment. He admits some teammates suffered from homesickness and he remembered how difficult that can be. He still missed his parents and two young siblings. Younger brother Jordan and sister Carrie are both hockey players and enthusiastic fans of their big brother.

In his early days in the billet, Jonathan found himself chowing down on sausage and sauerkraut. He realized his billet family would have accommodated his tastes and the nutritional requirements of a young athlete, but he was too shy to speak up. Older and wiser, Jonathan spoke to his Belleville billet family about his food preferences.

Like most athletes Jon realized that his diet affects his performance and was careful to eat appropriately, particularly at pre-game meals. This didn't mean gourmet dinners. Jon's favourite food is spaghetti, a good complex carbohydrate that gives him the energy he needs to play. With fifteen years of experience in housing hockey players, his billet parents are no strangers to feeding young athletes, even future NHL stars. Edmonton's Bryan Marchment once chowed down at the same table.

Life In Belleville

Even though the players have to earn a spot in August, the team had the players select school courses during the summer. Jonathan was in grade twelve and carrying a full courseload. School occupied most of Jonathan's non-hockey time. He had a free period in the morning and did his homework before class. The team had tutors but Jonathan preferred to go to teammates when he needed some help. There is usually someone who has taken the course and can lend a hand.

Jonathan learned that being a player means a lot off the ice. The team receives a lot of support from the community and the players like to give back. Jonathan enjoyed one of his bigger assignments. Along with the local police he participated in a drug abuse seminar for younger children. He also did some autograph sessions at the local mall.

The team doesn't forget its older fans and raked leaves for community members. Being the offensive kind of guy he is Jonathan bagged a lot of leaves. It was fun for the guys and a way of showing their appreciation to their fans. A Christmas charity project had Jonathan and the other Bulls warming up their vocal cords. What song would a group of young hockey players be singing? "All I Want for Christmas Is My Two Front Teeth."

Down Time

The league requires a lot of hard work but the team does try to provide some recreational events for its players. The team often hosts dinners for the players, or the whole team will go to a movie together. Jonathan tries to make friends with classmates. He thinks it's important to have some balance and that means interests and friends outside of hockey.

Looking Ahead

Jonathan came into the league with goals. He wanted to be an impact player and justify the faith his team demonstrated by drafting him fifth in the league. His rookie season was also his NHL Draft-eligible year and that thought did hover in the background. The NHL Draft is a big step towards Jonathan's dream of playing in the NHL and he hoped to make a solid impression. Ranked highly by Central Scouting, Jon headed into the second half of his rookie season in fine form for the June Draft. As Team Cherry's MVP Jon certainly showcased his talents at the 1998 Prospects Challenge. He caught the attention of the San Jose Sharks who snapped up the young forward twenty-ninth overall in the 1998 NHL Entry Draft.

Jonathan Cheechoo
Top Prospects Challenge,
February 1998
*Photograph courtesy of the CHL and Dan Hamilton \
Vantage Point Studios*

Final Words for Future Rookies

"Learn as much as you can. Don't get depressed if you are not playing as much as you would like. You just have to work through it. You have to increase your skill level and take advice from the veterans. Most important—go out and have fun. Sometimes it will be tough, but if you love the game, once you get in there and play the fun comes out."

Chapter 16

FAR FROM HOME: INTERNATIONAL PLAYERS IN THE CHL

Some players come further than others upon earning a spot on a CHL team. Canada's elite Junior league is graduating some top international prospects. The league limits the number of European players on the roster to two per team. With fifty-four teams in the league, that is still a high number of European players.

They are coming into the league by way of an Import Draft, held every year in the spring. Some players are not interested in coming to Canada but many do want to make the move and experience playing in this elite league.

Gregor Baumgartner, Laval Titans (Austria)

Gregor Baumgartner is living the Canadian dream. In June 1997 he was selected thirty-seventh overall by the Montreal Canadiens. The Habs are the winningest team in NHL history and, as one of the original six teams, hold a special place in Canadian hearts. Gregor grew up not knowing the NHL and now his biggest dream is to play there.

Born in Leoben, Austria, Gregor grew up in a country whose winter obsession was

Gregor Baumgartner
Laval Titans
Photograph courtesy of the Baumgartner family

169

downhill skiing. When it came to team sports, soccer was the big winner with young Austrians, Gregor included. Hockey was a casual sport which he got into by accident. It was raining, so he couldn't play soccer. His mother took him to the rink instead. Gregor liked what he saw. His parents got him some used skates and enrolled him.

Gregor's father and grandfather were enthusiastic soccer fans. If he were to become a professional athlete, that sport would have been their choice. They had reason to hope; when he was twelve Gregor was the top scorer in both soccer and hockey. Despite the national and family preference Gregor was hooked on Canada's game and decided to stick with hockey.

He played as much as he could. Packing a lunch, he would leave with his stick in the morning and come back at night. Gregor was not dreaming of being the next Bobby Orr or Maurice Richard. He didn't know who these icons were. The first NHL player that Gregor really heard about was Wayne Gretzky.

The Austrian hockey program is not divided the way the Canadian program is; players are grouped by age, not by skill level. Gregor admits this does decrease the quality of competition. The difference between the best and worst player is too big. As they got older, more players dropped out of the program and it became more challenging.

Gregor wanted to test his hockey talent and that meant some travel. His parents, humoring their son's obsession, allowed him to attend hockey schools all over Europe. A real test of parental commitment came when Gregor and his parents took a trip to Russia to see the hockey program there.

The family only stayed two and a half weeks. The situation was not very good. It was just after the Chernobyl nuclear disaster. Although they were staying at a top hotel, food was scarce. Gregor admits it was an eerie experience; there were whole generations missing. You saw babies and older people but not young children. The family packed up and headed back to Austria.

Gregor got turned on to the Canadian program when at age thirteen he attended a Peewee International Tournament held in Quebec. Gregor was a member of the Austrian National Team. In his first game he scored six goals. He was delighted until he found out about a deal Wayne Gretzky had with the Tournament officials. Gretzky had scored seven goals in a game at the Tournament and agreed that if a player ever surpassed that record they would get to meet the Great One. This was one of the few NHL players that thirteen-year-old Gregor knew, and he was terribly disappointed when he found out. He knows the coach would have let him have some extra ice time to make up the points.

The hockey was good and Gregor thought about coming over to Canada to play. Some Canadian teams also thought that would be a good idea. After the tournament a team in Red Deer, Alberta, invited the young Austrian to come play. During the Peewee tournament in Quebec Gregor had gotten to know the Canadian in charge of the Austrian National Team and he offered Gregor the chance to come and play in Quebec.

Canada was not Gregor's only option. He was also considering programs in Germany, the Czech Republic, and some other northern European countries. However, it seemed that most players were trying to get to Canada, so why take two steps? Canada was hockey country. When it came to choosing between Alberta and Quebec, Gregor decided to go with Quebec for two reasons: he had actually been there and his grandmother was French. He made the decision more easily than his parents.

They had some concerns about letting their fourteen-year-old son move to a foreign country. Gregor admits that he probably got to go because his parents were sure he would stay only a couple of weeks and then come home. Almost five years later Gregor's parents have stopped asking if he wants to come home.

Playing Canadian Hockey

Gregor admits when he came over he did not really understand the hockey system and he had never heard of the CHL. He was more concerned with getting on the ice than figuring out the system. When Gregor came over the first team he made was Bantam.

Bantam is a physical league and Gregor admits he was not prepared for the Canadian game. He got hit a lot and was being moved off the puck. Eventually he adjusted to the more physical play and got back into the game. The league was faster and the quality of the players was very high.

Living In Canada

Adjusting to Canada meant learning a new language. Gregor spoke a bit of English when he came but his billet family spoke French. Sign language got him through the early months and after about six months he was conversational in French.

When it came to school Gregor stuck with English since he could read English. The teachers were supportive. Gregor started out in grade nine but quickly picked up the pace. He finished grades nine, ten and eleven in two years.

The big thing Gregor noticed about Canada was the cold. It was a long, hard winter for the young Austrian but he got a warm jacket and coped. Culturally, Canada was different as well. Gregor was used to going to school at seven a.m. and being out by one p.m.; Canadians got up later and went to bed much later. Gregor also noted that driving is bigger in Canada, a sixteen-year-old being eligible to drive.

Playing NCAA

In his second year, Gregor was playing AAA Midget and doing well enough to be ranked in the top ten for the Major Junior Draft. By now he knew about the CHL and was anxious to earn a spot in the elite league. Unfortunately, no one realized until the last minute that as a European Gregor was not eligible for the QMJHL Draft. At fifteen he was too young for the Import Draft.

His dreams of the CHL frustrated, Gregor turned to the United States. He scored well on his SATs and got accepted at Clarkson University. Now sixteen, Gregor was the youngest player in the program. His early start in college earned him the nickname Doogie Howser.

The American program was a big change from Canadian hockey. The month of September was off-ice conditioning and there were only thirty-two games in the regular season. As the youngest player on the team Gregor was not seeing a lot of ice time. He felt that the program would not make him competitive with players seeing an eighty-game season so he decided to head back to Canada.

Gregor Baumgartner
Top Prospects Challenge,
February 1997
*Photograph courtesy of the CHL and Dan
Hamilton, Vantage Point Studios*

172

Gregor moved to Hull to play AAA Midget. His academic ambitions did not end when he left Clarkson; he enrolled at the University of Ottawa. During the season he also joined the Austrian National team for the World Junior Tournament. At the end of the season Gregor was finally old enough for the Import Draft. He was drafted second overall by the Laval Titans.

Playing In the CHL

Gregor was happy to finally get the chance to play Major Junior hockey. He thinks the CHL offers an incredible opportunity to develop your game. The long season helps players prepare for a career in hockey and it also provides a forum where players can show their talent to interested scouts. The scouts evidently found the young Austrian very interesting.

On Getting Drafted

Since living in Canada, Gregor has learned enough about the NHL to want to play here. He was excited when his draft day finally arrived. Gregory's parents had been to Canada several times and they knew how important this day was for their son. His second-round selection by the Montreal Canadiens was a big deal and it also had the potential of doubling the number of Austrians playing in the NHL.

Gregor spent two-and-a-half weeks at Montreal's camp. He was able to play a couple of AHL games before rejoining the Titans. The games were great experience and after fifteen years of carrying his gear around it was nice to have someone else responsible for it.

In Final Analysis

Gregor admits that some people are not thrilled to have Europeans playing in Canada

Gregor Baumgartner
Montreal Draft Prospect
Photograph Courtesy of the Baumgartner family

and they can be critical of the way he plays. Overall the teams and coaches have been supportive. When his game was not going well Gregor got a bit homesick, but he is happy with his decision to come to Canada to play hockey.

Elias Abrahamsson, Halifax Mooseheads

Elias is a long way from his home in Uppsala, Sweden. He is currently living in Rhode Island and playing with the Providence Bruins. He spent three years with the Halifax Mooseheads before being drafted by the Boston Bruins in the fifth round of the 1995 NHL Entry Draft.

Elias started playing hockey when he was seven. Despite high-profile NHL stars like Mats Sundin and Peter Forsberg, hockey was not a big sport in Sweden. When Elias was younger, soccer was the sport most kids grew up playing. Although there were a few Swedish players in the NHL, Elias did not grow up hoping to end up there.

He started to play hockey because it was fun and as he got older he realized that he was pretty good. The NHL was something he became more aware of when he was playing in Canada. In Canada players are divided by skill. In Sweden players are segregated by age. Admittedly many players drop out as they get older, so the level of competition goes up.

One difference Elias noticed right away in Canada is the prevalence of hockey. Everybody plays. There were approximately a thousand students at Elias's high school in Sweden but only about a dozen played hockey. He concedes that with the success of Team Sweden in the World Cup and their performance at the Olympics more young people will start to play. There have always been elite leagues in Sweden and the quality of players has been excellent, but hockey is definitely gaining a wider popularity.

Making the Move

When he was seventeen Elias decided that he wanted to do something different. He originally considered being an exchange student in France. A different option presented itself in the form of interest from a WHL team in Saskatchewan. The father of a friend knew someone in Saskatchewan and helped the team contact Elias. Although Elias did not really know anything about the CHL he liked hockey and was curious about in living in Canada.

The WHL team decided to pass on the young Swede but another team gave Elias a call. The Halifax Mooseheads were a new franchise in the CHL and they were hoping to add the Swedish defenceman to their roster. Before using their draft selection they wanted to know if Elias would be willing to relocate. He indicated that he was and the team drafted him. Not all European players are willing to relocate and some are not willing to stay. Teams try to make sure that players are interested and willing to adjust to life in another country.

Elias notes that players have to have the right attitude. Moving to another country means changes. You have to be prepared for that; expect to have to adapt to a different language and a different culture.

It is important to respect the community where you live. As Elias is quick to point out about his move to Halifax: "It was my responsibility to adjust, I was coming over here." After three years, Elias said he enjoyed living in Halifax and was happy to have improved his English.

When you are so far away from home you can miss it and get down. It is important for a player to try to stay positive. Listen, learn and be open to change. The one caution that Elias has for young European players is only come over if that is what you really want. Do not come to please someone else or because you feel pressured to.

The Import Draft

Elias feels that the quota of two foreign players per team is fair. It is after all the Canadian Hockey League. Swedish teams impose similar quotas on the number of foreign players in their leagues. Elias does think that the Import Draft will become more well-known and more popular in Europe. More players are aware of the opportunities in the NHL and want to come over and play.

Going to Camp

Going to your first training camp is always a nerve-racking experience. Doing it in a foreign country when you can only understand about one in twenty words can be downright scary. Elias was excited but apprehensive. Like any draftee, he was only guaranteed a trip to camp; to stay he had to earn a spot. With sixty other prospects competing for positions, it meant a lot of hard work.

The camp was held outside Halifax. The only other European at camp was from the Czech Republic. About half the players at camp were French-speaking and about half were English-speaking. Elias' English was marginally better but he has managed to improve both his French and English during his stint with the team.

Playing the North American Game

Elias admits that the North American style of hockey was different than he was used to. The camp was held at an Olympic-sized rink so

Elias did not have to adjust to the smaller ice surface right away. The first exhibition game had the team on NHL-sized ice. Elias found the smaller ice surface easier; as a defenceman he could get back faster and had a smaller area to cover.

The style of play was different; the North American game was much more physical. With everyone trying to earn a spot the exhibition games were pretty aggressive. At 6'3" and 216 pounds Elias had the size to play a physical game. It was an adjustment, but as Elias put it "he hacked back." With 278 penalties in his second season with the Mooseheads, it seems he learned pretty quickly how to play the Canadian way.

Living In Halifax

After making the team Elias headed for Halifax where he hooked up with his billet family. They did not speak Swedish, but sign language and patience allowed Elias to settle in without much difficulty. You miss certain things, but you learn to find substitutes. He also learned to use

Elias Abrahamsson – Halifax Mooseheads
Photograph courtesy of Terry Waterfield

the internet, which allowed him to read Swedish newspapers and e-mail friends.

The Canadian attitude towards meals was more casual than the attitude in Sweden. Elias was surprised by how much Canadians snack. Meal times are more fixed at home; in Canada people eat whenever they are hungry and they eat out a lot more. With the hectic schedule and frequent road trips Elias has picked up Canadian snacking habits.

Elias continued his education in Canada. He started out in grade eleven, but by the end of the year had enrolled in St. Mary's University. Elias took two or three courses each semester during his stint in Halifax. Although he did not enroll in any courses in Rhode Island he planned to look into correspondence courses over the summer.

When it comes to culture Elias found Canadians extremely friendly, very casual, often talking to strangers. It was definitely a welcoming attitude and Elias made a number of friends during his time here. The fan support and community interest was amazing; people really followed the team's progress. This was a new experience for Elias. He still tries to get back to Halifax during the summer for a visit.

Playing In the League

Elias likens Major Junior hockey to a job. You play or practice every day. The hockey in the league is very competitive and you really have to play hard. The schedule was much more rigorous than his schedule in Sweden.

Elias Abrahamsson – Halifax Mooseheads
Photograph courtesy of Terry Waterfield

When Elias came over he knew that CHL teams played a lot of games and that a lot of NHL players came from the league. In terms of exposure Elias admits it was a great showcase for the NHL draft. Although he did not grow up dreaming of the NHL, he was definitely thinking in that direction after spending some time in Junior. The season is long and it was sometimes tough to stay focused, but Elias played hard and was hopeful about the NHL Draft.

He did not attend the draft but returned home to Sweden for the summer. He found out he had been drafted when the Boston Bruins called him. It was a happy moment for the young defenceman.

Life After Junior

After three years with the Mooseheads Elias made the jump to the AHL. At twenty, he played with the Boston Bruin's farm team in Rhode Island. Elias credits his time in Halifax with preparing him for the lifestyle. The game schedule and travel time are very similar to his Junior days. He does concede that not having a curfew and having a salary is a pleasant change from Junior.

In Final Analysis

The CHL delivered on its promise to provide player development and exposure. Elias does not know if he would have ended up in the NHL if he had gone another route but he is glad to have had the opportunity to play Major Junior. Although he planned to get home to Sweden for the summer, his career plans were definitely in North America.

Pavel Rosa, Hull Olympiques (Litvinov, Czech Republic)

Anyone who saw the 1998 Olympics knows that hockey is a very popular game in the Czech Republic. That country is also the birthplace of some top NHL stars. When Pavel Rosa grew up, young players were not dreaming of NHL futures. Young Czech players wanted one day to play in the Czech Republic's elite senior league.

As a young boy, Pavel would often go to the rink to watch the Litvinov club. Litvinov boasts one of the top teams and Pavel was able to watch very talented players, including his personal idol, Robert Reichel.

Pavel's dream was to one day be a member of that team; that dream has changed. By the time Pavel was in his early teens the NHL was becoming popular in Eastern Europe. At least the top teams were; the only games televised in the Czech Republic were playoff games.

Pavel liked what he saw. His ambition became to follow in the footsteps of players like Robert Reichel and play in the NHL. Drafted in the second round of the 1995 NHL Entry Draft by the Los Angeles Kings, Pavel was well on his way to fulfilling that dream.

Pavel's father was an avid sports enthusiast and encouraged his two sons to pursue athletics. He played soccer but he encouraged his sons to play hockey. Although they played soccer and hockey when they were younger, Pavel and older brother Stanislav decided to go with hockey. In the city of Litvinov hockey seemed to be the most promising career choice.

Pavel began playing hockey when he was five years old. The Czech program is age-driven until players hit fourteen. It is tough to make the Junior "B" league. Players in this league range in age from fourteen to sixteen. When they reach sixteen they need to make the Junior "A" league. Players in this league are seventeen to nineteen.

Pavel was playing Junior "A" hockey when he caught the eye of Charles Henry, the GM of the Hull Olympiques. As an eighteen-year-old and already projected to be picked up in the June NHL Draft, Pavel had no interest in packing up and heading for Canada. His initial reaction was to say no to the move.

The plan was to get drafted, spend a few more years playing in the Czech Republic and then head to North America. This is a path other top players have taken. Dominic Hasek, Jaromir Jagr, and Robert Reichel all played in the Czech senior league before joining the NHL.

The Hull Olympiques GM was not willing to give up on such a promising young player. Although the CHL teams are allowed to draft players in the Import Draft there is no guarantee that the player will choose to come to Canada. Teams often try to feel out a player and get a commitment before drafting the player.

Henry called Pavel several times and eventually flew over for a visit. Pavel's agent arranged for him to speak with a player in the CHL. Pavel kept thinking about the offer and finally after two months of hesitation he said yes. Although he talked with his family and with his agent, the final decision was his alone. It is a decision he was glad he made.

Although many players choose the CHL for exposure that was not a real concern for Pavel. Litvinov is very well scouted. The Litvinov Club is the second largest contributor of young players to the NHL in the Czech Republic. Players like Robert Lang, Martin Rucinsky, Petr Svoboda and Petr Klima came from Litvinov to join the NHL. Pavel was drafted by the L.A. Kings in the June Draft before he came to Canada to join the Hull Olympiques.

179

Moving To Canada

Pavel arrived in Hull just in time to catch an exhibition game. Arriving directly from the airport, he did not play in the game. It was pretty rough; several fights broke out. Pavel's first thoughts were, "I am supposed to play in this?" but then he focused more on the game. It was different but he felt he could play in the league. He knew he was a good player and the players were his age.

He did not have time to settle in. He headed out almost immediately for the Kings' training camp. When he returned from camp it was time to start his CHL career. When he arrived back in Hull he got a bit homesick. It had finally sunk in that this was not a visit. He would be staying in Canada.

To help ease the transition for the young Czech player, the team arranged for Pavel to billet with the same family as the other Czech player on the team. The player was in his second year with the team and helped Pavel settle in and improve his English. Pavel also credits the family with helping him learn English. He learned English his first year with the team and became conversational in French in his second season.

Living In Canada

Winter in the Czech Republic means temperatures around minus five Centigrade. Pavel soon learned that was a good day in Canada. The temperature was a change but he just bought a warm parka. Now that he is living in Los Angeles, Pavel actually misses the changes in season and the snow.

Food was another adjustment Pavel had to make. Breakfast and lunch in the Czech Republic are very big meals. In Canada, the only big meal is supper. Back home a meal meant lots of meat or fish and cheese, usually breaded and fried with heavy sauces and gravies. Pavel admits he would not make a pre-game meal out of those foods but he did miss the home cooking.

Pavel did get a taste of home once in a while. His roommate had made some Czech friends in the city. The two young players would visit and get a chance to enjoy a Czech-style home-cooked meal.

In the Czech Republic, the cities are much smaller. Pavel could get across Litvinov in about twenty minutes. In Canada, the cities sprawl out and most people have cars. One pleasant change for Pavel was access to the regular season NHL games. He watched a lot of games during his first winter in Canada. He is a big fan of TSN. Now that he lives in the United States he watches ESPN but says that he prefers TSN. Hockey always comes first.

Playing In Canada

Pavel admits that playing in the CHL was a good decision. The season in the Czech Republic is only fifty-five games, recently increased from forty games. The CHL's longer season meant more ice time and helped Pavel prepare for the long NHL season.

The two biggest changes that Pavel faced playing in the CHL were a smaller ice surface and a more physical game. The smaller ice surface was great; it meant Pavel was always closer to the net. With 116 points in the 1996-97 season his being closer to the net was bad news for the other team.

The travel time in the league was another big adjustment. Pavel was used to short three to four hour trips and now the team was packing up for the fifteen-hour drive to Halifax. The first season was tough but Pavel eventually got used to the travel and sleeping on the bus.

The Memorial Cup

The first year that Pavel arrived in Hull he knew very little about the Memorial Cup. He was busy adjusting to the new league. At the start of the 1996-97 season he knew exactly what the cup was and what it

Pavel Rosa, No. 55 – Hull Olympiques
Photograph courtesy of Dan Hamiliton, Vantage Point Studios

meant to win. Since the team was hosting the tournament he also knew he would be making a bid for that coveted trophy.

It was a long and exciting year for the team and Pavel admits he wanted to win that cup as badly as any Canadian-born player. It was a tremendous victory for the team. Pavel had some special fans watching the tournament: his parents had made the trip from the Czech Republic to watch him play.

Life After Junior

The Memorial Cup victory marked the end of Pavel's Junior career. Unfortunately his NHL career got off to a slow start. The promising young winger was injured in a pre-season game against the Colorado Avalanche. The injury left Pavel sidelined for most of the season. It was a frustrating time for the young prospect but he knew he needed to give himself time to heal.

Cleared to return to the game late in the season, Pavel joined the IHL's Long Beach Ice Dogs. He had trained hard and was glad to be back in the game. Pavel joined the L.A. Kings' lineup in the 1998-99 season and is enjoying his first season in the NHL.

In Final Analysis

Pavel is glad he overcame his initial reluctance to join the Hull Olympiques. The two years he spent with the team were helpful. Pavel got to adjust the North American style game and he knows that will make his transition to the NHL smoother. He also met some really great people and polished his English. He has spoken with other young Czech players who are considering making the leap. He is happy with his decision and feels that choosing the CHL was a great move.

Pavel Rosa, No. 55
Hull Olympiques
Photograph courtesy of the Hull Olympiques

Chapter 17

ARE YOU TOUGH ENOUGH?

"It is a rough road that leads to the heights of greatness"

Lucius Annaeus Seneca

Adjusting to living away from home and coping with hockey, school, and community commitments are difficult enough but the league has a few other twists that can make for a tough transition. Coping with the demands of the game, the new environment and the pressure that comes with talent makes mental toughness imperative.

This chapter looks at some of the more difficult adjustments young players make pursuing the dream. Playing in the league means facing trades, media scrutiny and new environments. Some players share their experiences in facing these challenges. L.A. Kings' prospect Don McLean offers some advice on keeping focused and getting through the rough spots.

TRADE RUMOURS: TRADING IN THE LEAGUE

Like its big brother, the CHL league is a trading league. All three leagues have a January trade deadline but trades are common throughout the season. Trades are sometimes requested by players and sometimes initiated by team management. According to coach Parry Shockey pre-playoff trades are relatively common where players are aging out of the league and their teams will not be making a playoff run.

Former Vancouver Canucks and Kamloops Blazers coach Tom Renney indicated that trading can be a very difficult experience for a player. It means a new team mid-season, with a different coach and new teammates. The WHL covers four provinces and two states and that can mean a big move. Whatever the reason, Renney feels it is a coach's responsibility to make sure that the parents and player are aware of the possibility of a trade.

A Player's Perspective: *Larry Paleczny, Owen Sound*

Larry knew that players got traded but he didn't know he would be one of them. After all, he had a no-trade clause in his contract. Larry was just starting his second season with the Belleville Bulls when he was traded. His trade was a management decision and came without warning.

He was sleeping when his billet mother came knocking on the door saying he had a call from the coach. It was seven a.m. and the groggy player thought she was joking. She wasn't. The coach wanted Larry to come down to the rink around ten. That was Larry's first indication that something was brewing.

When he got to the rink his coach told him that he had been traded to Owen Sound. They called the Owen Sound coach and he spoke to Larry. He was enthusiastic about having Larry join the team and encouraged him to come immediately. Larry admits they would have given him some time but since his new team wanted him to play in a game that night he decided to go.

When he returned to his billet, he made some quick calls. First to his parents, then his agent and then to some teammates and friends to let them know about the trade. The players who were around came over to say goodbye. The quick move meant that Larry did not get a chance to say goodbye to everyone. He still keeps in touch with friends in the city and visits during the summer.

With the car packed up Larry hit the road and was heading out of Belleville by twelve-thirty p.m. His first stop was a brief visit with his parents in Kitchener before driving

Larry Paleczny, No. 19
Owen Sound Platers

Photograph courtesy of the Owen Sound Platers

through to Owen Sound. He went straight to the rink and suited up for his first game as a Plater. It was a bit of an adjustment playing with a new team. After the game he met his roommate and they went out to grab a bite before going home to meet his new hockey family.

He immediately hit it off with his new housemate and that made for an easier transition. The other players were welcoming; trades are common and there was no tension with a new player in the mix. The team arranged for him to finish out the semester by correspondence so he didn't lose any academic credits in the move.

Trading is a part of the league and in this case worked out well. Larry's new team was much closer to home and he was seeing more ice time. On the down side he went from a team that was leading the league to one that was much lower. Being traded is always an adjustment but Larry felt it was all part of growing as a player.

Despite being unprepared for the trade he never considered not reporting to his new team. He did not consider invoking his no-trade clause. He was a player the Bulls considered expendable and one Owen Sound really wanted. The trade worked out well for the young forward. Paleczny led his team in scoring at the end of the 1996-97 season with seventy-two points in fifty-nine games.

It is a pretty big day for a player when he wakes up a Bull and goes to bed a Plater. Usually the player has some advanced warning of a trade. The Owen Sound centre was pretty philosophical about his move noting that the only difference between trading now and trading in the NHL is that now you pack your suitcase and in the NHL you have to pack up your house.

Expansion Drafts: New Team, New Teammates

Being traded isn't the only way a player can end up with a new team. The CHL has been expanding in recent years (thirteen new teams in eight seasons) and those new teams need players. Jay Henderson learned this first hand when he was selected in the Expansion Draft by the Edmonton Ice.

The second-year veteran had to leave his team, the Red Deer Rebels, and head for Edmonton to join the Ice. Jay had to say goodbye to his teammates, billet family and friends hoping that he would quickly be making new ones. It was awkward at first being on a team full of strangers. Jay had to do some quick bonding but the team did start to gel.

Jay still got to see his old teammates—they were just on the opposite end of the ice. In his first game against the Rebels he had some difficulty adjusting. He admits he wasn't playing like his usual self.

Jay Henderson, No. 16 – Edmonton Ice
Photographs courtesy of the Dan Hamilton, Vantage Point Studios

Fortunately it was an exhibition game. By the time the regular season started it was back to business as usual.

Jay has stepped up as a leader on the fledgling team providing maturity and scoring talent. He finished out his first season second in scoring and led the team in the early months of their second season. His performance earned him an invitation to the WHL's All-Star game.

LIFE IN THE FISH BOWL: COPING WITH THE MEDIA

Major Junior teams are big news in their home cities and draft prospects are always news. Young players who join CHL teams can suddenly find themselves being written up in the local sports pages or interviewed on television. It can be fun to hear that you are the next big thing; it is not so fun to hear that you are a pylon with a stick.

Whatever the comments, players need to learn to cope with the media. One player admits that if the team is not doing well he stays away from the sports page. The writeup won't help his game and he concedes that it can hurt his confidence. Confidence is a big part of the game and performance can suffer when the news is negative.

One player has his own antidote for negative comments. He has a highlights tape. When he needs to get his head back in the game he watches the tape. Experienced players recommend that you filter information coming out of the media. To be effective you have to focus on your job—you go out and play hard. The proof of your ability is in your performance, not one sports writer's commentary.

Players point out that learning to deal with the media is a helpful part of the Major Junior experience. The media does not get kinder up the line. NHL players are frequently criticized in the media and from the stands. One player noted that even Wayne Gretzky is not immune. Whenever the "Great One" has a few games without a goal, speculation is loud and nasty.

Heckling does not always come from the opposing team's fans. Leafs fans have high expectations and the player who is not performing hears it loud and clear. Young players admit it can hurt to be heckled. When the crowd is chanting "You Suck" it impacts on your performance.

One player notes that the media has "big ears." No matter how friendly or casual the conversation you need to be careful what you say. A good guideline is never say anything you do not want to end up in the paper. The media can be looking for controversy and you have to be professional about your comments. This can be difficult. Occasionally a player is written up in the papers and knows that the story is one-sided. He wants to explain, but it's yesterday's news. There is more to hockey then the on-ice action; problems with management or coaches make great stories.

The local media is not the only thing that players need to be aware of. In a small community, word of mouth can be as damaging to a player's reputation as the local sports page. Players' actions on and off the ice are always a focus of comment. Local communities are often supportive of the team and have expectations of the players. Players recognize that their position on the team makes them role models for younger players; this is a serious responsibility.

It can be a pain; you do not get a break. You do not get the chance to have a bad day or be cranky. If you make a mistake it is news. If you make a nasty remark out of frustration or in the heat of the moment it could be tomorrow's headline. As a player you always have to be aware of your behaviour. Everyone matures through experience but young players have to do their learning front and centre in the glare of the spotlights.

CULTURE SHOCK: LIVING IN A NEW COMMUNITY

Playing Major Junior may mean moving miles or even provinces away from home. Some players need to make more of an adjustment. One of the biggest adjustments for young players is in the QMJHL where language differences can create difficulties for players. With four teams in the Maritime provinces more English-speaking players are going to Quebec and French players are ending up in English communities.

Randy Copely, Granby Predateurs/Cape Breton Screaming Eagles
When it came time for this young prospect to be drafted he had some serious thinking to do. Randy knew that living in a French community would be difficult for him. He did not speak French and was not sure how he would adjust. He and his agent decided to write to the teams in completely French communities and request that they not choose Randy in the upcoming draft. Some teams do have bilingual communities and Randy was hoping to restrict his draft options to those cities.

Unfortunately, the Granby Predateurs were just not willing to pass on such a promising young player. They drafted Randy in the second round of the QMJHL Draft. Once the draft was done Randy did not consider not going. Hockey was too important to him. At sixteen he packed up and headed for Quebec.

The camp was easier than he anticipated. A number of Maritime players were at the camp so there was no shortage of English-speaking players. Once the cuts were made only six English players remained on the team; then two were traded to Halifax. One player was from Newfoundland, another was from Norway and the third was a native player from Montreal.

On the ice, drills were done in both French and English. With a predominantly English NHL, most players were anxious to improve their English. The team meetings were in French. Randy admits to sitting through the meetings trying to look serious and being completely clueless. He would talk to players after the meeting for a quick summary. Randy also had one-on-one meetings with the coach, who was bilingual.

Although most of the French players could speak some English they tended to chat in French. That cut Randy out of casual conversations and the banter that is part of team bonding. It was not an intentional exclusion, the players were just French-speaking. If Randy asked questions players spoke to him in English. Some players were pretty fluent but many were struggling and conversation ended up being forced.

The father of Randy's billet family was bilingual and made an extra effort with him. He realized that Randy was having a difficult adjustment and took time to chat with him.

Living in a French community made common tasks more complicated. When he went shopping Randy would often get frustrated because he could not even ask simple questions without a hassle. After going through the same drawn-out and confusing process every time he wanted to pick up a few things, Randy gave up. If he could not pick it out and bring it to the cash it stayed in the store.

Randy did pick up some phrases during the season. He had taken French in school but he was uncomfortable with his pronunciation. He tried to take French in the English-speaking school he attended but it was too advanced.

The frustration wore on Randy and in January of his rookie season he was ready to call it quits. His parents told him to get a flight, he packed his bags and called the GM to tell him that he was going home. The decision was a difficult one. Randy really thought that would be it for his hockey dreams. He wasn't thinking about a trade or coming back next year. He truly believed it was over for him.

When the GM got the call he was concerned and urged Randy to stay until they could talk things over. Randy waited and spoke with the coach and the GM. Randy admits he is not a talkative guy and the coach did not realize how fed up he was until he was packed to leave. After talking things out he decided to finish out the season.

Randy's year in Granby was difficult for him. He kept playing but he was not really enjoying the experience. Near the end of the season he heard some news that gave him some hope. Granby was moving and the Maritimes were a strong possibility. Randy spent the summer glued to the radio as reports went back and forth on whether the team would come to Cape Breton. It was finally announced that the Predateurs had become the Cape Breton Screaming Eagles. Randy was excited. As a native of Cape Breton he would be playing to the home crowd.

Randy Copley, No. 32
Cape Breton Screaming Eagles
*Photograph courtesy of the Cape Breton
Screaming Eagles*

Despite a rocky start Randy is glad he stuck it out. He had a lot of fun the first year in Cape Breton. He received invitations to both the QMJHL All-Star game and the CHL's Prospects Challenge. His stellar performance earned him a second round selection by the New York Rangers in the 1998 NHL Draft.

In his third season Randy once again headed to Quebec. He joined the Rouyn-Noranda Huskies as part of a trade. No longer a rookie in the league, Randy was more comfortable about going to play in Quebec. He appreciated how adaptive French-speaking players on the Cape Breton Eagles were and planned on making the same effort in Rouyn-Noranda.

Randy realized it would be difficult but he was excited about the move. He was extremely pleased to be joining a team that was playing well and had high aspirations for the post-season. The move went well for the young prospect. The team and the other players have been helpful and supportive of their new English-speaking teammate. Most players are bilingual and most of the on-ice work is in English.

Derrick Walser, Rimouski Oceanic

New Glasgow's Derrick Walser never had the opportunity to return to Nova Scotia. He played in Quebec for three years. Derrick made the trip to Quebec when he joined the Beauport Harfangs. Unilingual when he joined the team, Derrick has become conversational in French.

The initial adjustment was a difficult one. When he was drafted by the Beauport Harfangs he was scared by the prospect of living in a French community. He wasn't going to be making the trip alone. Halifax native Don MacLean would also be going to Beauport. The two Nova Scotians were the first English players to join the team.

With a billet family that spoke only French, Derrick was reduced to charades when it came to communicating. He did manage to bond with his family. Hockey has its own language and he would often watch games with his new family. When it came to meals Derrick would accompany them shopping and help them choose foods that he liked.

A nearby English school allowed Derrick to continue his education while he was with Beauport. When he began playing for Rimouski he continued his education by correspondence with the help of a tutor. The community is French. If he wanted to pick something up at the store or get gas he had to learn how to speak French. The constant immersion in the language made picking it up easier. It was definitely tough. You have to be able to laugh at yourself and since you don't get any of the jokes that is the only laughing you will be doing.

You need to respect the other players and be willing to adapt. The first month is the worst; you have to be prepared to be frustrated. When it came to playing, many of the players were at least conversationally bilingual. Derrick admits sometimes he had to make a little extra effort to make sure he was understood.

Derrick has no regrets about making the decision to play in the league. It's about loving the game and making the commitment to hockey. French players have to adapt to the NHL and English players have to adapt to the French communities in the QMJHL.

BEFORE YOU GIVE UP: MAKING IT

Don MacLean, Hull Olympiques/ Los Angeles Kings

Don MacLean knows first hand how tough it can be in the CHL. The Kings prospect has been traded three times during his stint in the QMJHL. He was with Derrick when they first headed for Quebec. The former Hull Olympiques player spent four months in Los Angeles with the Kings at the start of the 1997-98 season. That was a long way from Halifax and it was not always an easy road.

Playing In Quebec

Don left home to play in Beauport of the Quebec league. His view on the distinct society—definitely. Quebec is different, the language and the culture are an adjustment and for a young player away from home for the first time it can be very tough. Don's view is simple: players have to go to Quebec with the right attitude. You are going to the province to play, and you have to be willing to respect and adapt to the culture. Don admits it is tough but he credits the experience with being a great character builder.

Getting Through the Homesickness

Major Junior players usually leave home when they are sixteen or seventeen. You are leaving your family, your friends and your lifestyle behind. Don admits he spent lots of nights on the road wondering if he was crazy, if he should just go home. At times it was very tempting. Now that he is starting his professional career, Don is glad he never gave in to that temptation.

To help him make it through those early months he cut up the season. His girlfriend came to visit early in the season, then he had Christmas at home to look forward to. Whatever was coming up became the count-down. It helped to make the long season more bearable. He just focused on getting through a couple of weeks at a time.

Playing In the League

When Don started the season with Beauport he was doing pretty well. He was seeing regular ice time, scoring lots of points. Unfortunately, in the second half of the season he started spending more time on the bench. The lack of ice time left him frustrated. Don was a top player; sitting on the bench was not something he was used to. During the second half of the season he managed only one goal and one assist.

One caution Don has for young players is that there are variables you cannot control, so be prepared. The quality and depth of the team, the coaching style, the location you are drafted to—it can leave you feeling powerless and frustrated. As a player you have to focus on what you control, focus on your game, on learning and improving, on preparing yourself for the future.

In addition to the homesickness and the lack of ice time Don was having problems with his billet family. He has had some very good families during his time in Major Junior but occasionally you run into situations where things just do not click.

All things considered it was adding up to a tough rookie season. Don admits he would get upset and depressed. Sometimes sheer stubbornness kept him going. He had made a commitment to the team and to himself when he came to play and he was staying.

Don credits family and friends with helping him through some of the rougher spots. Older brothers Randy and Rob were both hockey players although neither played Major Junior. They would call to chat and help Don keep his spirits up. He also ran up a pretty hefty long distance bill keeping in touch with his girlfriend back in Nova Scotia.

When Don sounded particularly close to the end of his rope on the phone he could usually count on his father, Bill, to show up for a visit. He also had some friends on the team who were going through the same adjustment. Derrick Walser and Brad Hartland had made the trip to Quebec with Don. Being down was not something that you talked about in the locker room but it helped having a couple of close friends going through the same experience.

Traded . . . Once, Twice, Three Times

Don had no problem making the team. His problem was staying with the team. During his time in the Junior league Don wore three different jerseys; in fact he wore three jerseys in one year. No matter what reassurances you are given, Don's advice is be prepared to be traded.

The first trade came only a few days after he returned from his first camp with the Kings. Don barely had time to unpack in Beauport before being traded to the Laval Titans. He might as well have left his suitcases packed because in December of that season he was traded to the Hull Olympiques.

It is difficult to join a new team mid-season and it was Don's third team in a season. As unsettling as trades are, they are part of the game and you have to have a positive attitude. Since Hull is a bilingual community there were a number of English-speaking players and that helped make the transition easier. The fact that the team went on a winning streak just after Don joined also helped him settle in fairly quickly. Since the trade resulted in a Memorial Cup win for Don it was a very good trade.

Don MacLean,
Hull Olympiques
Photograph courtesy of the Hull Olympics

The Glamour Game?

Don scoffs at the view that hockey is all glamour and fun. It is an extraordinary amount of work and sacrifice. On a typical day in Junior he would leave the house at 7:30 a.m. to go to school and get home at 8:00 p.m. after practice. Those were the days he wasn't at a game or on the road.

The reality is that it is not really a fun lifestyle. Your friends are hanging out and going to parties on weekends; you are at home by ten or eleven p.m. for your curfew. Even if you do not have a curfew you are probably so tired you don't want to go out anyway. Sometimes you get frustrated and want to stay out late, but you need to make responsible decisions.

For elite players, the need for discipline does not end with the season. Training during the summer is a vital part of the game. Players are expected to come to camp in August in shape.

The life is physically and emotionally demanding but Don thinks it is just part of the growing-up process. The difference is that junior players do it a few years earlier than their peers who put it off until they head to university.

Worth It?

During his stint with the Los Angeles Kings, the team did a little roadtrip from Ottawa to Montreal. It was a route that Don knew very well from his days in the QMJHL. He had bussed it back and forth on this same route over and over again. During those long drives he had sat in the dark and contemplated the game and his future, and occasionally questioned his decision to pursue hockey as a career.

On this trip, he had no questions and no doubts. He was where he wanted to be and it had definitely been worth the effort. He has no regrets about his Junior career. Sticking it out when it was tough helped him mature as a person and as a player. He admits it was a rough road and that he is still not firmly established. But Don MacLean loves hockey; for him it was and is a dream worth chasing.

ON A FINAL NOTE

Donovan Nunweiller chased his dream into the CHL and Don MacLean is leaving the league behind for a professional career. Like thousands of other young athletes these players have chosen the CHL as part of their hockey experience. It is an intense and often demanding experience.

Making the team is a tough task and getting on the roster is no guarantee of a successful year. There are difficult times, hard work and doubts providing insight into their roles and responsibilities.

The dream of playing NHL hockey takes players through the long bus rides and into the countless arenas. These young hopefuls sit down at strangers' tables and make lifelong friends. The players share a common dream and they know the odds are against them.

What players do have in the CHL is the opportunity to play a game they love, to improve their skills, to meet new people, to experience new communities, to travel in Canada and sometimes beyond and to chase that dream of playing NHL with all their passion and ability. However his Major Junior career ends, the player will know that he pursued his dream diligently through a system with a long and important history in Canadian hockey.

References

MEETING
THE
CHL TEAMS

THE QUEBEC MAJOR JUNIOR HOCKEY LEAGUE (QMJHL): THE TEAMS

The Robert LeBel Division	The Frank-Dilio Division
Drummondville Voltigeurs	Baie-Comeau Drakkar
Hull Olympiques	Cape Breton Screaming Eagles
Acadie-Bathurst Titans	Chicoutimi Sagueneens
Rouyn-Noranda Huskies	Halifax Mooseheads
Shawinigan Cataractes	Moncton Wildcats
Sherbrooke Castors	Quebec Remparts
Val d'Or Foreurs	Rimouski Oceanics
Victoriaville Tigers	

CHICOUTIMI SAGUENEENS

History of the Team: This team is a veteran in the league having started play in the 1973-74 season. Has made Memorial Cup Tournament appearances in 1991, 1994 and 1997 but has yet to bring home the hardware. Division Champions in 1987-88, 1990-91, and 1993-94. Also won the President Cup as Playoff Champions in 1990-91 and 1993-94.

Rink Information: The Sagueneens call the George Vezina Centre home. It seats 3,926, total capacity 4,649.

Notables: Jimmy Waite, Eric Fichaud, Alain Cote, Guy Carbonneau, Marc Bergevin, Stephane Morin, Felix Potvin, Marc Bureau, Michel Bolduc.

The City: With a population of 64,100 Chicoutimi is one of the most important urban centres in the Saguenay region. Chicoutimi means "there where it is deep." This is a reference to the waters of the Saguenay river.

DRUMMONDVILLE VOLTIGEURS

History of the Team: The Voltigeurs hit the ice in the 1982-83 season. Made Memorial Cup Tournament appearances in 1988, and 1991. Led the Frank-Dilio division in the 1985-86 season.

Rink Information: The Marcel-Dionne Centre is home to the Voltigeurs, with a total capacity of 3,622 and seats for 3,038.

Notables: Rene Corbet, Steve Duchesne, Claude Boivin, Daniel Dore, Yanic Dupre, Jose Charbonneau, Denis Chasse.

The City: Located in the heart of Quebec, Drummondville is on the Saint-Francois river. The city is midway between Montreal and Quebec. Founded in 1812 and named for its British Governor, the city began life as a military outpost but soon became a major industrial centre.

DRAKKAR DE BAIE-COMEAU

History of the Team: The Drakkars are an expansion franchise and hit the ice in the 1997-98 season.

Rink Information: The Henry-Leonard Centre is home to the Drakkars. Seats for 2,797 and a total capacity of 3,042.

Notables: This newcomer to the league has yet to graduate players to the NHL.

The City: This northern city is one of the smaller cities in the league with a population of 26,700. Located on the Bay of St. Lawrence, this city has access to hydroelectric power that has turned the city into a major industrial centre.

LES REMPARTS DE QUEBEC

History of the Team: This team began life in 1990 as the Beauport Harfangs and was moved to Ste-Foy in 1997, re-named the Quebec Remparts.

Rink Information: The PEPS-Universite Laval is home to the Remparts, with a total capacity of 2,425 and seats for 1,975.

Notables: Eric Daze, Marcel Cousineau, Matthew Barnaby, Don MacLean, Yannick Tremblay, Patrick Cote, Christian Lafamme, Jean-Yves Lecroux.

The City: Ste-Foy is the home to the oldest French language university in North America, University of Laval. This city is a near neighbour to Quebec city.

CAPE BRETON SCREAMING EAGLES

History of the Team: The newly renamed Screaming Eagles began life as the Bisons. The Granby Bisons entered the league in 1981-82 and in 1995-96 became the Granby Predateurs. The team was moved to Cape Breton, Nova Scotia at the beginning of the 1997-98 season. Granby was Memorial Cup Champion in 1996. The team won the John-Rougeau Memorial Trophy in 1986-87 and 1995-96. The team also won the President Cup in 1995-96.

Rink Information: Vacated by the Cape Breton Oilers, the 4,916-seat Centre 200 arena is home to the new Screaming Eagles.

Notables: Stephane Richer, Patrick Roy, Pierre Turgeon, Daniel Lacroix, Jason Doig, Eric Desjardins, Philippe Boucher, Jesse Belanger, Andre Racciot Jr.

The City: Located on Cape Breton Island, Sydney is the industrial centre for the island and the city is home to the University College of Cape Breton. Sydney is a port city located on the Atlantic Ocean.

HALIFAX MOOSEHEADS

History of the Team: The team joined the league as an expansion franchise in the 1994 season. The 1997-98 season was the team's most successful as they fought to a heartbreaking game seven loss in the division finals.

Rink Information: The Mooseheads occupy the 9,811-seat Halifax Metro Centre. The nineteen-year-old rink is the staging area for most major events in the city. It is shared with the CIAU's St. Mary's Huskies.

Notables: Jean-Sebastien Giguere, Éric Houde.

The City: The capital of Nova Scotia, Halifax is dominated by an ice-free harbour. With a population of 114,000 this historic city is a centre for tourism and government. The city is also home to King's College, Dalhousie University, Mount St. Vincent University and St. Mary's University.

HULL OLYMPIQUES

History of the Team: This 1996-97 Memorial Cup winning team started in the league in the 1973-74 season. The team made three Memorial Cup bids before finally bringing the Cup home in 1997. Won the President Cup as playoff leaders and the Jean-Rougeau Memorial Trophy as regular season leaders in 1985-86, 1987-88, 1994-95 and 1996-97.

Rink Information: Home to the Olympiques is the Arena Robert Guertin with a seating capacity of 3,506 and a total capacity of 4,906. During the 1997-98 Memorial Cup Tournament you can bet the arena was filled to capacity.

Notables: Luc Robitaille, Martin Gelinas, Ted Bulley, Benoit Brunet, Glen Sharpley, Sylvain Turgeon, Karl Dykhuis, Jeremy Roenick.

The City: Founded by an American loyalist, this city, population 60,900, sits on the Ontario border directly across the river from Ottawa. The city's close proximity to English-speaking Ontario has given the city a bilingual nature.

ACADIE-BATHURST TITAN

History of the Team: A grandfather in the league, this original franchise team hit the ice in the 1969-70 season. The team has been known as Laval National, Laval Voisins, Laval Titan and more recently Titan du College Francais de Laval. Laval won the Jean-Rougeau Memorial Trophy in 1982-83, 1983-84, 1993-94, and 1994-95. They also won the President Cup in 1983-84, 1988-89, 1989-90, and 1992-93. Laval has made five Memorial Cup Tournament

Appearances but has yet to bring home the Cup. The team was moved to New Brunswick in the 1998-99 season bringing the total for Maritime teams up to four.

Rink Information: The K.C. Irving Regional Centre is the new home of the Titans and seats 3,500 fans.

Notables: Mario Lemieux, Vincent Damphousse, Claude Lapointe, Don Audette, Gino Odjick, Sandy McCarthy, Robert Sauve, Mike Bossy, Jocelyn Lemieux, Yvon Vautour, Jean-Jacques Daigneault.

The City: Bathurst is a mining and industrial centre located on the Baie des Chaleurs. The bilingual nature of the city is a reflection of the Acadian heritage of many of the residents.

MONCTON WILDCATS

History of the Team: The team joined the league in the 1995-96 season starting life as the Moncton Alpines and in 1996-97 became the Moncton Wildcats.

Rink Information: The Moncton Coliseum is one of the larger venues in the league. There is seating for 6,598.

Notables: A relative newcomer to the league, this expansion franchise has yet to graduate players to the NHL.

The City: With a population of 57,010 this Maritime city is a home to Acadian francophones and English-speaking descendants of loyalists, making for a diverse cultural and language mix. The city is home to a French language university, the University of Moncton.

RIMOUSKI OCEANIC

History of the Team: The team entered the league in 1969 as the Sherbrooke Castors and in 1982 moved to St. Jean. Changed to the Lynx before moving to Rimouski and becoming the Rimouski Oceanic in 1995. The team won the President Cup in 1974-75, 1976-77, 1981-82 and the Jean-Rougeau Memorial Trophy in 1974-75, 1975-76, 1979-80, 1981-82. In 1977 the Sherbrooke Castors made a bid for the Memorial Cup but lost out to the New Westminister Bruins.

Rink Information: The Rimouski Oceanic call the Colisee de Rimouski home. The arena seats 4,299 and has a total capacity of 5,062.

Notables: Francois Leroux, Benoit Hogue, Christian Proulx, Yves Sarault, Jason Doig.

The City: Rimouski means "land of the Moose" in Micmac and is located on the St. Lawrence river. Today this city is an important wood processing centre. With a population of 33,100, Rimouski is considered to be the administrative capital of Eastern Quebec.

ROUYN-NORANDA HUSKIES

History of the Team: The team entered the league in 1982-83 as the Verdun Jr. Canadiens. The team became the Ste. Hyacinthe Lasers in 1989 and made the move to Rouyn-Noranda in 1996 when it was renamed the Huskies. In its first season in the league Verdun won the President Cup and made a bid for the Memorial Cup.

Rink Information: The Huskies call the Dave Keon Arena home. There is seating room for 1,996 fans and a total capacity of 3,500.

Notables: Joel Bouchard, Jimmy Carson, Pat LaFontaine, Daniel Marois, Patrick Poulin, Denis Savard, Martin Brodeur, Claude Lemieux.

The City: Rouyn-Noranda is in the Abitibi region of Quebec, near the Ontario border. The city is neighbours with Val-d'Or. Originally established after the discovery of large gold and copper deposits, the city remains an important ore processing centre with a population of 26,450.

SHAWINIGAN CATARACTES

History of the Team: This team was an original franchise, entering the league in 1969. They have remained in Shawinigan but have played as the Bruins and the Dynamos. The team lead the Frank-Dilio division in 1982-83, 1983-84, and 1984-85. In 1984-85 the team won the President Cup as playoff leaders and went to the Memorial Cup.

Rink Information: Home for the Cataractes is the Jacques Plante Arena which seats 3,700 and has a total capacity of 4,200.

Notables: Sergio Momesso, Dominic Roussel, Jean Francois Quintin, Patrick Lebeau, Enrico Ciccone.

The City: Shawinigan is a hilly town whose name means "portage at the peak" in Algonquian. Founded in 1899, this city was laid out by the Shawinigan Water and Power company who were attracted by the strong currents of the Sainte-Maurice River and the fifty-metre falls. This city of 21,300 supplies electricity to Montreal.

SHERBROOKE CASTORS

History of the Team: The team started life as the Ducs of Trois-Rivieres in 1969. In 1973 the team's name was changed to the Draveurs. The team won the President Cup and Jean-Rougeau Memorial Cup in the 1977-78 and 1978-89 seasons as the Draveurs. The name was changed again in 1991 when the team became the Sherbrooke Faucons. In the 1992-93 season the Sherbrooke Faucons won the Jean-Rougeau Memorial Trophy. In the 1998-99 season the team became the Castors.

Rink Information: The Castors call the Palais des Sports home. This arena seats 4,328 and has a total capacity of 5,328.

Notables: Normand Dube, Claude St. Sauveur, Reggie Lemelin, Mario Lessard, Richard Mulhern, Gord Donnelly, Sean McKenna, Francois Leroux, Stephane Beauregard, Jose Theodore, Denis Chasse.

The City: With a population of 77,629 this city is one of the main urban centres in the Estrie region of Quebec. Located southwest of Montreal the city is nicknamed "the Queen of the townships" and straddles the Saint-Francois River. The city is home to the University of Sherbrooke, which was founded in 1952.

VAL D'OR FOREURS

History of the Team: The team is a relative newcomer to the league. The Foreurs hit the ice in 1993-94 as an expansion franchise.

Rink Information: The Foreurs are at home in the Palais des Sports which seats 2,140 with a total capacity of 3,500.

Notables: A relative newcomer to the league, Val d'Or has yet to graduate players to the NHL but with prospects like Robert Luongo it won't be long.

The City: The Valley of Gold sprang to life with the discovery of the precious mineral in 1922. The city of 24,100 is still an important mining centre. Val-d'Or is located near Rouyn-Noranda in northern Quebec.

VICTORIAVILLE TIGERS

History of the Team: In the 1982-83 season the Longueuil Chevaliers hit the ice. The team was moved to Victoriaville and renamed the Tigers in 1987-88. As the Chevaliers the team managed a President Cup win in 1986-87. The Tigers also won the Jean-Rougleau Memorial Trophy in the 1989-90 season.

Rink Information: The Tigers are at home in the Amphitheatre Gilbert-Perreault. The arena seats 2,050 and has a total capacity of 2,700.

Notables: Alexandre Daigle, Stephane Fiset, Jean-Jacques Daigneault, Yves Racine, Donald Brashear.

The City: Established in 1861, the city was named after Queen Victoria. A near neighbour to Drummondville, the city is midway between Montreal and Quebec. With a population of 37,000, the city owes its development to the forestry and steel industries.

THE ONTARIO HOCKEY LEAGUE (OHL): THE TEAMS

EASTERN CONFERENCE		WESTERN CONFERENCE	
East	*Central*	*Midwest*	*West*
Belleville Bulls	Barrie Colts	Erie Otters	London Knights
Kingston Frontenacs	Mississauga Ice Dogs	Brampton Battalion	Plymouth Whalers
Oshawa Generals	North Bay Centennials	Guelph Storm	Sarnia Sting
Ottawa 67's	Sudbury Wolves	Kitchener Rangers	Sault St. Marie Greyhounds
Peterborough Petes	St. Mike's Majors	Owen Sound Platers	Windsor Spitfires

BARRIE COLTS

History of the Team: The team is a relative newcomer to the league having only started to play in 1995/96 season. This new franchise has already managed to produce a couple of first-round NHL Draft selections in Alexander Volchkov and Daniel Tkaczuh.

Rink Information: The team is stabled in the Barrie Molson Centre which opened in 1996. The Colts are the only hockey tenants of this facility which has a seating capacity of 4,195.

Notables: Brad Brown.

The City: Barrie is a small city located about an hour and a half north of Toronto. It is surrounded by farming communities. The city has a population of over 90,000 and is growing rapidly.

BELLEVILLE BULLS

History of the Team: The Bulls entered the league in 1981 as an expansion franchise.

Rink Information: The Bulls call the Yardman Arena home. This arena seats 3,257.

Notables: Mike Hartman, Darren McCarthy, Marty McSorley, Rob Pearson, Dan Quinn, Troy Crowder, Bryan Marchment, Scott Thornton, Craig Billington, Dan Cleary.

The City: Belleville is located on the Bay of Quinte at the mouth of the Moira River in Eastern Ontario. Belleville is centrally located just two hours from Toronto and two and a half hours from Ottawa. The city has a population of 37,243 and is home to Albert College and Clarke College.

PLYMOUTH WHALERS

History of the Team: The franchise succeeded in making the OHL an international league in 1988 when the Detroit Junior Red Wings entered the league. In 1994 when Compuware purchased the Hartford Whalers the team was renamed the Detroit Whalers. The team took back-to-back division titles in 1995 and 1996. They entered the 1997-98 season as the Plymouth Whalers.

Rink Information: The team plays in the new Compuware Sports Arena, a facility that contains two ice surfaces and seating for 4,300. The arena is shared with seven youth teams also sponsored by Compuware.

Notables: Jamie Allison, Kevin Brown, Eric Cairns, Bryan Berard, Pat Peake, Sean Haggerty, Todd Harvey.

The City: The Township of Plymouth is located in Michigan and has a population of 23,646.

ERIE OTTERS

History of the Team: The team began life in Hamilton, changing its name three times during its stint in the city: Tiger Cubs, Red Wings, Fincups. They were still the Fincups when the team moved to St. Catharines in 1976. The Fincups returned to Hamilton in 1977 but at the end of the season moved to Brantford to become the Alexanders. The team remained there until 1984 when they once again returned to Hamilton this time as the Steelhawks. The team moved and became the Niagara Falls Thunder in 1988 before moving south of the border to Erie in 1996.

Rink Information: The team occupies a 5,542-seat arena at the Erie Civic Center.

Notables: Shayne Corson, Brad Dalgarno, Dave Gagner, Mike Lalor, Keith Primeau, Bob Probert, Brad May, Dave Hannan, Greg DeVries, Ethan Moreau.

The City: The city of Erie is the only Pennsylvania port on the Great Lakes and is considered the cultural hub of the tri-states area. The city, with a population of 800,000, boasts two colleges and universities.

GUELPH STORM

History of the Team: Originally the Toronto Marlboros, the team was moved to Hamilton in the 1989-90 season. The team remained there until 1991-92 when it was renamed and relocated as the Guelph Storm. The Toronto Marlboros won the Memorial Cup six times (1929, 1955, 1956, 1964, 1967, 1973 and 1975). The Guelph Storm led the league in 1996 but lost out at the Memorial Cup Tournament.

Rink Information: The team calls Guelph Memorial Gardens home. The arena provides 3,950 seats to Storm fans.

Notables: Todd Bertuzzi, Steve Thomas, Mike Prokopec, Jeff O'Neill, Sean Burke, Peter Zezel, Steve Thomas, Bill Berg, Ken Belanger.

The City: Guelph is a small city with a population of 93,400. It is located in the heartland of Southern Ontario and surrounded by the Great Lakes. The city is home to the University of Guelph and has a fast growing economy.

KINGSTON FRONTENACS

History of the Team: The team celebrated twenty-five years as the Kingston Frontenacs in 1998. The team was originally called the Montreal Junior Canadiens but became the Kingston Canadiens in the 1974-75 season. Nine years later the team changed the franchise's name to the Kingston Frontenacs. As the Montreal Junior Canadiens the team won back-to-back Memorial Cups in 1969 and 1970.

Rink Information: The Frontenacs have operated out of the Kingston Memorial Centre for their entire twenty-five-year history. The arena boasts seating for 3,079 fans. The team is hoping to have a new arena in the near future.

Notables: Ken Linesman, Kirk Muller, Mike O'Connell, Jay Wells, Tim Kerr, Neil Belland, Mike Gillis, Bernie Nicholls, Chris Gratton, Brett Lindros, Chad Kilger, David Ling, Jeff Chychrun.

The City: Kingston is located where Lake Ontario empties into the St. Lawrence River in Eastern Ontario. The city is renowned as the freshwater sailing capital and is the gateway to the Thousand Islands. The city has a population of 141,200 and is home to Queen's University, St. Lawrence College and the Royal Military College.

KITCHENER RANGERS

History of the Team: The Rangers moved from Guelph in the 1963-64 season. The thirty-five-year-old team was Memorial Cup Champion in 1982. They were league champions in 1981 and 1982.

Rink Information: The Rangers are the city's main tenants at the Kitchener Memorial Auditorium. This rink has a capacity for 6,700 Rangers' fans.

Notables: Paul Coffey, Larry Robinson, Allan MacInnis, Brian Bellows, Bill Barber, Steven Rice, Shawn Burr, Mike Hough, Wayne Presley, Todd Wariner, Boyd Devereaux.

The City: The Kitchener/Waterloo area is a community of picturesque towns and villages, and a number of Mennonite communities. The population of this area is 269,663 and it is home to the University of Waterloo and Wilfred Laurier University.

LONDON KNIGHTS

History of the Team: This team has been in London since its 1967 founding.

Rink Information: This team has called the London Ice House home for its thirty-year history. The rink seats 4,573 but there is room for 5,573.

Notables: Brad Marsh, Darryl Sittler, Dino Ciccarelli, Brendan Shanahan, Rick Green, Tim Taylor, Jason Allison.

The City: The City of London is located in Southern Ontario. With a population of 325,437 this city is also home to the University of Western Ontario.

NORTH BAY CENTENNIALS

History of the Team: The team began life as the St. Catharines' Blackhawks but was moved in the 1976-77 season to Niagara Falls. The team was renamed the Flyers. In 1982-83 the team came to North Bay and was renamed the Centennials. The Cents won the OHL Championship and made a Memorial Cup bid in 1994.

Rink Information: The team plays out of the North Bay Memorial Gardens. The arena has a seating capacity of 3,523 with a standing room capacity of 4,025.

Notables: Nick Kypreos, Mark LaForest, Andrew McBain, Paul Gillies, Derian Hatcher, Kevin Hatcher, Darren Turcotte, Bill Houlder, Vitali Yachmenev, Mike Gartner.

The City: North Bay is the hub of Ontario's Near North. It is a fishing centre located on the shores of Lake Nipissing. The city of 56,000 has a sizable French community.

OSHAWA GENERALS

History of the Team: The team was founded in 1937-38 by General Motors. The team was owned for a brief period in the 60s by the Boston Bruins; the current owners took control of the organization in 1967. The team has a record twelve OHL league titles and four Memorial Cup wins, 1939, 1940, 1944 and more recently in 1990.

Rink Information: The Generals play in the Oshawa Civic Auditorium built in 1966. The facility seats 3,411 and is shared with the Oshawa Legionnaires.

Notables: Bobby Orr, Jason Arnott, Rollie Melanson, Rick Middleton, Eric Lindros, Charlie Conacher, Dave Anderychuk, Charlie Huddy, Kirk McLean, Derek King.

The City: The city of Oshawa is located on Lake Ontario about forty-five minutes east of Toronto. It is an industrial and automotive centre. The population is 132,500.

OTTAWA 67'S

History of the Team: Founded in 1967, the team chose Canada's Centennial Year as its name. The 67's won the Memorial Cup in 1984. They also finished first in their division in 1978, 1982, 1983, 1984, 1996 and 1997.

Rink Information: The Ottawa 67's call the Ottawa Civic Centre home. The rink seats 10,575 and the team shared space with the Ottawa Senators until their new arena was completed.

Notables: Brad Shaw, Darren Pang, Bill Clement, Doug Wilson, Bobby Smith, Denis Potvin, Andrew Cassels, Mike Peca, Shean Donovan, Alyn McCauley.

The City: Ottawa is the capital city and federal seat of government in Canada. Located on the provincial border with Quebec this picturesque city has a population of 313,987. Ottawa has a large bilingual population and is home to Carleton University, Algonquin College and the University of Ottawa.

OWEN SOUND PLATERS

History of the Team: The team began life as an expansion franchise in Guelph in 1982-83 and relocated to Owen Sound in the 1989-90 season. The Platers brought home the Memorial Cup in 1986.

Rink Information: The team calls Henry Lumley Bayshore Community Centre home. The arena seats 2,640 and has a capacity of 3,640.

Notables: Kirk Maltby, Rob Zamuner, Kirk Muller, Wayne Primeau, Andrew Brunette, Jamie Storr, Scott Walker, Kerry Huffman, John McIntyre, Alek Stojanov.

The City: Owen Sound is a small community with a population of 21,674. It is nestled in the valley of the Sydenham River on Georgian Bay in Southern Ontario.

PETERBOROUGH PETES

History of the Team: The Petes were established in 1956. They were OHL Champions in 1958-59, 1971-72, 1977-78, 1978-79, 1979-80, 1988-89, 1992-93. They were Memorial Cup winners in 1978-79 and hosted the tournament in 1996. This team has not missed the playoffs in twenty years.

Rink Information: Peterborough Memorial Centre has a seating capacity of 3,929.

Notables: Steve Yzerman, Bob Gainey, Tie Domi, Jason Dawe, Mike Ricci, Chris Pronger, Luke Richardson, Stan Jonathan, Larry Murphy, Rick MacLeish.

The City: The City of Peterborough lies on the banks of the Otonabee River. It is the commercial centre of a wide farming and recreational area. The city has a population of 67,823.

SARNIA STING

History of the Team: This team made a big move to join the OHL. The team started life as a QMJHL franchise in 1969-70 and moved to the OHL in 1981 where they became the Cornwall Royals. The team was moved to Newmarket in 1992 and finally to Sarnia in 1994-95.

Rink Information: The team plays out of the Sarnia Sports & Entertainment Centre. The arena has seating for 5,000 fans.

Notables: Doug Gilmour, Dale Hawerchuk, Jim Kyte, Owen Nolan, Rob Ray, Joe Reekie, Mathieu Schneider, Mike Stapleton, Ray Sheppard, Rick Tabaracci.

The City: Sarnia is located about sixty miles northeast of Detroit and west of London. With a population of 69,657 it is the largest city on Lake Huron.

SAULT STE MARIE GREYHOUNDS

History of the Team: Joined the OHA in 1972-73 season and in 1996-97 celebrated twenty-five years of Junior Hockey. The team was the Memorial Cup winner in 1993.

Rink Information: The team plays out of the Sault Memorial Gardens. The Gardens seat 3,687 and will accommodate 3,950.

Notables: Wayne Gretzky, John Vanbiesbrouk, Ted Nolan, Paul Coffey, Jeff Beukeboam, Ron Francis, Adam Foote, Rick Tocchet, Rob Zettler, Bob Probert.

The City: Sault Ste Marie, often called the Sault (pronounced Soo) is located in the heart of the Great Lakes and is separated from Michigan by the St. Mary's Rapids. The city has a population of 81,476.

SUDBURY WOLVES

History of the Team: This team began life as the Barrie Flyers. The team was moved to Niagara Falls in 1960-61 and finally to Sudbury in 1972-73 where they became the Wolves.

Rink Information: The Wolves make their home in Sudbury Arena. The arena has 4,760 seats and accommodates 5,760.

Notables: Pat Verbeek, Jeff Brown, Brandon Convery, Jason Bonsignore, Dale Hunter, Paul DiPietro, Craig Duncanson, Rory Fitzpatrick, Mike Hudson, Chris Kontos, Ken McRae, Glen Murray, Mike Peca.

The City: Sudbury is the largest centre in northeastern Ontario. Located near Lake Ramsay in the Canadian Shield, Sudbury is famous for mining nickel and copper. The city of 92,000 has a large francophone community and is home to a bilingual university and a French college.

WINDSOR SPITFIRE

History of the Team: The team was granted an OHL franchise in the 1975 season. The Spitfires were the OHL Champions in 1988 and went on to the Memorial Cup tournament.

Rink Information: The team calls the Windsor Arena home. This 4,300-seat facility was built in 1924 and is located in downtown Windsor.

Notables: Adam Graves, Todd Gill, Darryl Shannon, Darrin Shannon, Brad Smith, Ed Jovanoski, Jamie Storr, Jason York, Dave Roche, Roland Melanson, Pat Jablonski.

The City: Located on the U.S. border, Windsor is a near neighbour to Detroit, MI. Like Detroit the city is a major industrial centre.

TORONTO ST. MIKE'S MAJORS

History of the Team: This team re-joined the OHL in 1997-98 after leaving the league in 1962. The team was a powerful force in hockey, winning four Memorial Cups (1961, 1947, 1945, and 1934) during their tenure in Junior.

Rink Information: The team calls Maple Leaf Gardens home; the facility seats 15,783 fans.

Notables: Frank Mahovlich, Red Kelly, Ted Lindsay, Tod Sloan, Tim Horton, Dave Dryden, Gerry Cheevers, Joe Primeau, Dave Keon, Bobby Bauer, Fleming Mackell.

The City: With a population of over four million, Toronto is the largest city in Canada. The city is home to the University of Toronto, York University and Ryerson University. The team shares the city with the NHL's Toronto Maple Leafs.

MISSISSAUGA ICE DOGS

History of the Team: The team is a new franchise and hit the ice in the 1998-99 season. The Ice Dogs get their name and logo from owner Don Cherry's pet pooch Blue.

Rink Information: The franchise will be starting life in a new facility. The 5,300-seat facility will boast two NHL-size ice surfaces and be named the Hershey Centre after a major sponsor.

Notables: Hitting the ice in 1998-99, this franchise will look forward to sending players to the NHL.

The City: Located just west of Toronto this city boasts a population of 480,170. The city is also home to the Erindale campus of the University of Toronto and Sheridan College, Mississauga campus.

BRAMPTON BATTALION

History of the Team: The Brampton Battalion made their OHL debut in the 1998-99 season.

Rink Information: The new team play in a new arena, the Brampton Family Entertainment and Sports Centre. The facility seats five thousand and has four ice surfaces.

Notables: The league newcomer will have to wait a few years to graduate alumni to the NHL.

The City: Brampton is located just northwest of Toronto. The rapidly-growing city is a near neighbour to the Icedogs and St. Mike's Majors.

THE WESTERN HOCKEY LEAGUE (WHL): THE TEAMS

WEST DIVISION	CENTRAL DIVISION	EAST DIVISION
Kamloops Blazers	Calgary Hitmen	Brandon Wheat Kings
Kelowna Rockets	Kootenay Ice	Moose Jaw Warriors
Portland Winter Hawks	Lethbridge Hurricanes	Prince Albert Raiders
Prince George Cougars	Medicine Hat Tigers	Regina Pats
Seattle Thunderbirds	Red Deer Rebels	Saskatoon Blades
Spokane Chiefs		Swift Current Broncos
Tri-Cities Americans		

BRANDON WHEAT KINGS

History of the Team: The team has a twenty-nine-year history beginning in 1967. The Wheat Kings have made eighteen playoff appearances and have two league championships, the first in 1978-79 and more recently in 1995-96.

Rink Information: The team plays in Keystone Centre, which seats 5,008.

Notables: Chris Osgood, Ron Hextall, Jeff Odgers, Ray Ferraro, Brad McCrimmon, Wade Redden, Mike Leclerc, Bryan McCabe, Trevor Kidd.

The City: Brandon is the only Manitoba team in the WHL. It is a relatively small city with a population of 38,567 but provides ample educational opportunities. Brandon is home to Brandon University and Assiniboine Community College.

CALGARY HITMEN

History of the Team: Newcomers to the WHL, the Hitmen's first season was 1995-96. The distinctive name comes from part-owner Brett "the Hitman" Hart.

Rink Information: This fledgling team has a prestigious rinkmate in the NHL's Calgary Flames. The 18,742-seat Canadian Airlines Saddledome is home to the Hitmen.

Notables: This team is too young to have sent any players to the NHL.

The City: Calgary enjoys its status as one of Canada's major cities with a population of 828,516. The large population reflects a booming petroleum-based economy. The city is home to the University of Calgary, Southern Alberta Institute of Technology, and Mount Royal College.

KOOTENAY ICE

History of the Team: The Edmonton Ice joined the league in 1996 as a new franchise. The team was moved to Cranbrook and renamed the Kootenay Ice in the 1998-99 season.

Rink Information: The team has new digs at the 1,600-seat Cranbrook Memorial Arena.

Notables: Jay Henderson.

The City: Located in the Kootenay Mountain range, Cranbrook is a scenic city located near the famous Radium Hot Springs and Kootenay National Park. The city is a tourist and recreational haven.

KAMLOOPS BLAZERS

History of the Team: This team is a grandfather in the league with a thirty-year history. Starting as the Estevan Bruins, the team has been know as the New Westminster Bruins, the Kamloops Jr. Oilers and finally in 1984 became the Kamloops Blazers. The team has certainly blazed across the Western league with eleven league championships under its belt and three recent Memorial Cup wins in 1995, 1994 and 1992.

Rink Information: To catch these players you need to grab one of the 5,122 seats available at the Riverside Coliseum.

Notables: Scott Niedermayer, Craig Berube, Rudy Poeschuk, Doug Bodger, Shane Doan, Darryl Sydor, Andy Moog, Dean Evason, Todd Ewen, Paul Krause, Mark Recchi, Jarome Iginla.

The City: Located in the interior of the province, Kamloops is a relatively young city, having been incorporated in 1973. The city grew quickly and now boasts a population of 69,653. It is home to the University College of the Cariboo.

KELOWNA ROCKETS

History of the Team: While the NHL teams appear to be moving south of the border, this team has headed north. The team joined the league in 1991-92 in Tacoma, Washington and moved to Kelowna, B.C. in the 1995-1996 season.

Rink Information: The team is currently operating out of the Kelowna Memorial Arena which has a seating capacity of 1,855 and maximum capacity of 2,500. The team is planning a move into a new 6000-seat facility.

Notables: Michal Grosek, Michal Sykora, Ray Schultz.

The City: It appears that 1973 was a big year for B.C. cities. Like its northern neighbour Kamloops, Kelowna incorporated in 1973. It is slightly bigger than Kamloops with a population of 75,950. Located close to the American border this city is home to Okanagan University College. With its warm summer temperatures the city has been dubbed the Four Seasons Playground.

LETHBRIDGE HURRICANES

History of the Team: In its twenty-nine-year history the team has been through a number of names including Winnipeg Jets, Winnipeg Clubs, Winnipeg Monarchs, Calgary Wranglers, until becoming the Lethbridge Hurricanes in 1987. The team won the league championship in 1997.

Rink Information: After a number of moves the Hurricanes have settled into the 5,027-seat Sportsplex.

Notables: Gerald Diduck, Jayson More, Jamie McLellan, Chris Phillips, Mike Vernon.

The City: The most southern of the Alberta WHL cities, Lethbridge has a population of 60,974. It is also home to the University of Lethbridge and Lethbridge Community College. This city is a well-known mining centre and is located just north of the Montana border.

MEDICINE HAT TIGERS

History of the Team: The Tigers were founded in 1970 and are two-time Memorial Cup winners. The first win was in 1986-87 followed by a success in 1987-88.

Rink Information: A new arena was built in 1970. This 4,050-seat arena replaced one destroyed by fire in March 1969. The Tigers are the major tenant but share the facility with a men's recreational hockey league and the Oldtimers Hockey League.

Notables: Lanny MacDonald, Trevor Linden, Chris Osgood, Kelly Hrudey, Pete Peeters, Rob Neidermayer, Don Murdoch, Morris Lukowich, Bob Bassen, Murray Craven.

The City: Located near the Saskatchewan border, this city has a population of 43,625. Players interested in advancing their education can attend Medicine Hat College. The city is a centre for manufacturing and the distribution of agricultural products.

MOOSE JAW WARRIORS

History of the Team: The Winnipeg Warriors hit the ice in 1980 and in 1984 became the Moose Jaw Warriors. Despite seven playoff appearances the Warriors are still chasing a league title and a chance at the coveted Memorial Cup.

Rink Information: The Warriors call the Civic Centre home. This arena seats 2,845 and has a total capacity of 3,146.

Notables: Kelly Buchberger, Lyle Odelein, Theoren Fleury, Mike Keane, Darryl Laplante.

The City: It was a big move for the Winnipeg team as they relocated to a much smaller city. Named after Moose Jaw Creek, Moose Jaw has a population of 33,593. Home of "Mac the Moose," this city is an industrial centre. It is also home to the Moose Jaw Wild Animal Park and hosts the Saskatchewan Air Show every summer.

PORTLAND WINTER HAWKS

History of the Team: The team started life far north of its present location. In 1966 the Edmonton Oil Kings entered the CHL and in 1976 it packed up and headed to Portland. The Portland Winter Hawks became the first American team in the league. The team was league leader three times, twice as the Edmonton Oil Kings and once as the Portland Winter Hawks. It won the Memorial cup in 1983.

Rink Information: The team's home arena is the 10,016-seat Memorial Coliseum, with an alternate in the 17,141-seat Rose Garden.

Notables: Ray Ferraro, Dave Babych, Adam Deadmarsh, Steve Konowalchuk, Cam Neely, Mark Messier, Glen Wesley, Brad Isbister.

The City: Portland is the most southern member of the WHL. This major American city enjoys its status as Oregon's largest city with a population of 450,777. It is one of the largest cities in the league. The city is also home to the University of Portland, Bassist College, Concordia College and Cascade College.

PRINCE ALBERT RAIDERS

History of the Team: The Raiders entered the league in the 1982-83 season and the next year they were league champions. In 1985 they brought home the Memorial Cup.

Rink Information: The Raiders call the 3,102-seat Comuniplex home.

Notables: Ken Baumgartner, Kevin Todd, Pat Elyniuck, Dave Manson, Mike Modano, Richard Pilon, Byron Dafoe.

The City: This northern Saskatchewan city is located on the North Saskatchewan River and is near Price Albert National Park. Prince Albert is a lumber centre and has a population of 34,181.

PRINCE GEORGE COUGARS

History of the Team: With a twenty-five-year history, the Cougars are a solid presence in the league. However, they weren't always in their present location. When they entered the league in 1971 the team was the Victoria Cougars. The team became the Prince George Cougars in 1994. They were the league champions in the 1980-81 season.

Rink Information: The team calls the Prince George Multiplex 5,582-seat arena home.

Notables: Russ Courtnall, Micah Aivazoff, Grant Fuhr, Geoff Courtnall, Wade Flaherty.

The City: This city has the distinction of being the northernmost in the league. With a population of 69,653, Prince George is also home to the University of Northern British Columbia and the College of New Caledonia.

RED DEER REBELS

History of the Team: The Rebels entered the league four years ago and since then have managed an impressive three playoff appearances.

Rink Information: The 5,735-seat Centrium is home base to this young team.

Notables: Terry Ryan, Darren Van Impe. Mike McBain, Peter Lepoutillier.

The City: Located between Edmonton and Calgary, this much smaller neighbour has a population of 58,134. Red Deer has a long history, having been incorporated in 1913.

REGINA PATS

History of the Team: This team has an impressive twenty-eight-year history with the league, retaining the same name and same location. Even more impressive is an eighty-year history in junior hockey making the Regina Pats the oldest Junior Hockey Club in the world. There was a brief leave of absence from 1968 to 1970. This absence didn't slow the team down. They were league champions in both 1973-74 and 1983-84. Their long history is evident in their 1925 and 1930 Memorial Cup wins and their staying power is evidenced by another Cup in 1974.

Rink Information: The Pats play out of the nineteen-year-old 6,000-seat Regina Agridome promoted as "Showtime at the Dome."

Notables: Robert Dirk, Brent Fedyk, Jeff Friesen, Stu Grimson, Kevin Haller, Mark Janssens, Jeff Shantz, Mike Sillinger, Esa Tikkanen, Josh Holden, Derek Morris.

The City: With a population of 179,178 this city is the capital of Saskatchewan. Named after Queen Victoria this city is proud of its pioneer spirit. The city is located on a fertile plain. Regina is home to the University of Regina.

SASKATOON BLADES

History of the Team: With a hefty thirty years in the league this team has managed twenty-five playoff appearances. The team has remained in Saskatoon unplagued by name changes and moves.

Rink Information: To catch this team you need to get one of the 11,306 seats available in Saskatchewan Place.

Notables: Wendel Clark, Randy Gilhen, Brian Glynn, Joey Kocur, Curtis Leschyshyn, Brian Skrudland, Grant Jennings, Kevin Kaminski, David Brown, Kelly Chase.

The City: With a population of 186,058, Saskatoon is a major city. It is also home to the University of Saskatchewan.

SEATTLE THUNDERBIRDS

History of the Team: The team entered the league as the Vancouver Nats in 1971. Their next stop was Kamloops where they played four years as the Chiefs before moving to Seattle. After experimenting with the name Breakers the club settled down as the Seattle Thunderbirds in 1985.

Rink Information: The team calls Key Arena home. This facility seats 11,500 hockey fans and opened on October 30, 1995.

Notables: Ryan Walter, Petr Nedved, Glenn Anderson, Brent Severyn, Chris Joseph, Brent Fedyk, Stewart Malgunas, Shawn Chambers, Tim Hunter, Dody Wood , Patrick Marleau.

The City: Just south of the Canadian border this port city, known for its coffee and grunge rock, provides a strong American base for the CHL. Only two hours from Vancouver, snow is rare (but the ice is always in!). Seattle is the largest city in Washington and home to the University of Washington.

SPOKANE CHIEFS

History of the Team: In 1982 the Kelowna Wings entered the league. In 1985 they flew South to Washington State and became the Spokane Chiefs. The team has managed eleven playoff appearances and one league championship in 1995-96. They also took home a Memorial Cup in 1991.

Rink Information: This is the Chiefs' third year at home in the Spokane Veterans Memorial Arena. This arena seats 10,528 hockey fans.

Notables: Pat Falloon, Brent Gilchrist, Jason Podollan, Trevor Kidd, Valeri Bure, Jon Klemm.

The City: Spokane is located near the B.C. border below Kelowna. This American city boasts a population of 177,196 and is home to Gonzaga University and Whitworth College.

SWIFT CURRENT BRONCOS

History of the Team: As the team with the smallest population base this is the little team that could. Except for twelve seasons in Lethbridge the team has been in Swift Current since 1967. The team has managed three Western League championships and a Memorial Cup win in 1989.

Rink Information: The Broncos call the Centennial Civic Centre home and are the major tenants of this 2,239-seat facility.

Notables: Bryan Trottier, Dave "Tiger" Williams, Terry Ruskowski, Dave "the Hammer" Schultz, Brian Spencer, Joe Sakic, Geoff Sanderson, Trent McCleary, Sheldon Kennedy, Dean McAmmond.

The City: With a population of 15,000, this is the baby of the league. Despite its little league size this team draws a big league crowd and with an average of two thousand fans per game. This city is home to Cypress Hills Regional College.

TRI-CITY AMERICANS

History of the Team: This team is a thirty-year veteran of the WHL. They have made twenty-three playoff appearances and were twice league finalists. This team continues to chase a league championship and Memorial Cup berth.

Rink Information: To catch this team you will need one of the 5, 861 seats at the Tri-Cities Coliseum in Kennewick.

Notables: Stu Barnes, Scott Levins, Bill Lindsay, Olaf Kolzig.

The City: The smallest of the American WHL cities with a population of 42,155, Kennewick is located near the border of Oregon and Washington.

217

About the Author

Tracy McPhee comes from the small community of River Bourgeois, Cape Breton (which, the author attests, is an absolutely beautiful place to grow up). She has a business degree and law degree from Dalhousie University. Currently living in Toronto, Tracy practises law in the areas of labour and employment with McMillan Binch. She is an avid and indiscriminate reader and boxes regularly at Florida Jack's Boxing Club. The author enjoys going to the occasional Leafs' game at the ACC and cheers for the Leafs . . . unless they are playing the Montreal Canadiens. This is her first book.

To order more copies of

Chasing the Dream:
A Player's Guide

send $19.95 plus $5.05
to cover GST, shipping and handling to:

GENERAL STORE PUBLISHING HOUSE
Box 28, 1694 Burnstown Road
Burnstown, Ontario, Canada K0J 1G0
Telephone: 1-800-465-6072
Facsimile: (613) 432-7184
URL: http://www.gsph.com

VISA and MASTERCARD accepted